Wise Talk Wild Women

WiseTalk WildWomen

by Gwen Mazer with portraits by Christine Alicino

COUNCIL OAK BOOKS • SAN FRANCISCO • TULSA

COUNCIL OAK BOOKS

WWW.COUNCILOAKBOOKS.COM

ORDER@COUNCILOAKBOOKS.COM

PUBLICITY@COUNCILOAKBOOKS.COM

ISBN-13: 978-1-885171-87-0

ISBN-10: 1-885171-87-0

LIBRARY OF CONGRESS CATALOGING-IN-PUBLICATION DATA

Mazer, Gwen.

  Wise talk, wild women / by Gwen Mazer, with portaits by Christine Alicino.

    p. cm.

  ISBN-13: 978-1-885171-87-0 (hardcover : alk. paper)

  ISBN-10: 1-885171-87-0 (alk. paper)

  1. Middle-aged women—United States—Psychology. 2. Baby boom

generation—United States. I. Alicino, Christine. II. Title.

  HQ1059.5.U5M39 2007

  305.244'20973—dc22

                    2006102764

Designed and edited by Carol Haralson, Sedona, Arizona

Printed in Canada

Wise Talk Wild Women

Wise Talk Wild Women

The wild woman is gifted with a permanent and internal watcher, a knower, a visionary, an oracle, an inspiratrice, an intuitive, and a listener who guides, suggests and urges vibrant life.

With wild woman as our ally, leader, model, teacher, we see not through two eyes, but through the eyes of intuition, which is many-eyed.

CLARISSA PINKOLA ESTÉS, *Women Who Run With the Wolves*

The idea for this book began with my thoughts, feelings, and questions about being a woman in her sixties at the beginning of the twenty-first century. In the community where I grew up, I experienced older people who were not encumbered by age. One such person I was especially fond of was a member of our church. This woman must have been "old" when I was a little girl, but she practiced yoga, meditated, traveled, and told tales of fascinating places. I remember her always having something cheerful to say. Two of my great-grandparents lived to be a hundred. Even when he was well into his nineties, my grandfather's conversation continued to be as deep and illuminating as ever. He was very wise. I remember being in the garden with him on a night filled with stars when I was a little girl. He said, "I want you to remember that you can fly as high as the stars." This was a wonderful thing to hear as a young African American girl. Not until I was in my fifties did I realize the depth of that gift and the impact it had on my life. It embedded the idea that I could do anything I set my mind to, that I had choice in the matter.

I did not choose for myself the things that for many people mark the passage of time. I did not pursue a traditional working career, and in my marriages I consciously chose not to have children. I was an entrepreneur, and I operated essentially on my own schedule. Age seemed not to touch me.

And then everything happened at once. My mother, who had been extremely active into her mid-eighties, became ill and despondent; her life unraveled. I came down with pneumonia, and my brother was diagnosed with cancer. None of us had ever been ill, so this was a huge shock. My brother and I regained our health, and after my mother's death I began to think seriously about what being older meant. I looked at images that were supposed to represent women of my age. As I observed how the media defined us, I felt we were being stirred into a single demographic pot and spoken for by others. So much emphasis, especially in advertising, seemed focused on the value of youth and the need to appear young by any means possible. Young women worried about being old at thirty, just when they were gaining the tools to create meaningful lives. I looked into the cultural mirrors held up to women my age in television, advertising, and cartoons, and I saw elders, crones, fearful seniors, women fading invisibly on the edges of life. I did not see myself in those mirrors. On the contrary, I felt excited, vibrant, sexual, and curious, with rising energy for the quests of this new phase of my life.

I read Betty Friedan's *Fountain of Age,* in which she examines the phenomena of aging and retirement, and her feelings about being treated as if she were no longer vital. The perception from the media is that we are all going to be ill; we are going to need drugs; we are going to end up in care facilities; more and more of us will suffer dementia. Friedan brought the good news instead that fewer than 5 percent of Americans ever have Alzheimer's, that nursing home residence among people sixty-five and over is declining. According to the Centers for Disease Control and Prevention, in 1999, only eleven people per thousand between the ages of sixty-five and seventy-four lived in care facilities. I was very reassured by Friedan, and by Deepak Chopra. In his book *Ageless Body, Timeless Mind,* which became my bible for health and wellbeing, he describes three distinct ways to measure our age: chronologically (by the calendar); biologically (through physical signs such as organ function); and psychologically (by how old we feel). This clearly supported my own sense that age was not simply one thing, a number.

As I considered this, I felt a rising determination to find and converse with women who were growing successfully into the next stage of their lives, women who could serve as mirrors for our wisest selves and as signposts for those coming behind us. These women would span a broad spectrum of experience, having engaged life in many different ways. I began to gestate a series of questions that would form the background for this tapestry of conversations. What experiences were common among us? What had dictated our life choices? Who were we now, and how did we see our futures?

Choosing the women I would talk with was an organic process. I knew I wanted to interview Jean Houston and Barbara Marx Hubbard. I was intrigued with their thinking and inspired by what they had written. As I talked about the idea for this book, other women's names began to pop up. I didn't know about Keiko Fukuda, but I was fascinated when I heard about this woman in her nineties, reared traditionally in Japan, who had achieved double red belts and still actively taught the martial arts. How did she manage to do what she was doing? When I asked her about aging in our interview, she said, "Oh, I have too much to do to think about that now. I'll worry about those things when I grow old."

Keiko Fukuda exhibited traits that I would find common among the women I talked with. Each was her own individual. Each danced to her own drum. Even if she had tried to force herself into a cultural mold, her individuality and need to create kept popping out. Each one needed to create a life and an identity, an expression in the world, and each one seemed to find her own purpose, her own center. They could not be damped down. They were wild women in the truest sense.

One of the most crucial things the women shared was the ability to operate from intuition, and many believed this to be more and more important as they grew older. Many felt their spirituality and their intuition to be entwined. There is a difference between the inner voice, which I like to describe as a quiet whisper, and the loud voice of the mind or ego that is chattering away with opinions and ideas, what we did and what we didn't do, what we said and what we didn't say. When we begin to discern between the two, our minds can clear. The sediment settles to the bottom, and we start to see the wisdom we've gleaned from our life experience. Inner listening—and trusting and following what we hear—is the most important skill we can cultivate. The wise woman within will never lead us astray. If there is any one thing that I would most love for readers to take away from this book, it is the power of intuitive listening, visible in the lives of the women I interviewed.

As Dolores Huerta says, "We need to be out in the world." Then we get a sense not only of ourselves but also of our place in the scheme of things and our power to create for the good of all. Some of the women I spoke with knew from childhood what they were going to do in the world; others stumbled into their paths; still others were thwarted in their initial choice but found another of equal value. Glady Thacher wanted to be an artist, but she married and had several children. Still, that creative energy was bubbling, and eventually it found an outlet; her career was not intentional. Belva Davis, on the other hand, hid from a chaotic childhood in a fortress of books and film until the day she simply woke up, said, "I'm going to have a life," and intentionally went about creating one. Donna Eden turned a difficult early marriage, a serious illness, and a gift for perceiving energy into a lifework of healing. Jo Hanson rejected the fundamentalist Hillerite sect of her upbringing and found her way to the Hawaiian spiritual practice of Huna.

For all the women, turning sixty had meaning. A shorter time was left, and there was a lot they wanted to do. They were conscious of the need for change in the world. Living a fully integrated life and putting something good into the world became primary goals. This is something that seems to be happening more and more with women in their fifties, sixties, and seventies. Barbara Marx Hubbard says we are evolving as a species, and that women of this age are leading the way.

The women I spoke with knew that the authentic self evolves over time. In the words of Mimi Silbert, the criminologist who established a whole new model for restoring society's throwaway people to productive lives, "even people who are considered the problem have within them everything that's needed to become the solution. In order to find your own strengths, there has to be the weight of responsibility and ownership on you." Someone could come out of a terrible childhood and have dreadful experiences as a young person and rise above them early. Someone else could be angry about it for decades. That anger is going to show on her face and in her body language and in the way she interacts with people. The anger may not even be conscious. It may be an energy that creates antagonistic relationships and circumstances. But with the slow effort toward inner knowing comes the assimilation of experiences, and with that comes authenticity and personal power.

The personal power you encounter in this book is power that comes from the inside, from the core. Some women are afraid their power could diminish the power of others—their husbands, their children. There is nothing to fear because the power that comes from within nurtures and liberates others. It is inauthentic power that needs to make others feel small in order to make oneself feel large.

Authentic power does not come from the way we look or the things we have—things don't make us what we are. And yet personal presentation can add to presence and a sense of authenticity. Sometimes a person, when she sees herself in another way, becomes empowered. As an image consultant, I deal with women on issues of esteem and well-being, finding the authentic self. Most women don't really see themselves physically. I put a woman in front of a mirror and say, "Look at the length of your neck and the breadth of your shoulders and the way you hold yourself. This is the shape we have to work with. This is the canvas. Your body is the canvas." We are fortunate if, like Olga Murray, we have mothers who encourage us early in our lives to see what is strong and lovable about our bodies. But most of us hold all kinds of thoughts, conscious and unconscious, about what we don't have and what we do have and what we wish we had. I have heard women who were seeing their own beauty for the first time say, "I can't handle that. I can't handle that much attention. I'm used to being in the background." Every woman has her own special beauty and it calls for us to embrace our authentic selves. When we take on personal power we have to be responsible.

Our bodies change. As Veena Merchant said, "One day I realized men were not going to turn around and go 'Wow' anymore." Beate Prilio said, "I've become the woman of the second look."

But there is liberation in this as well. Those who attend to the changes in their bodies don't get stuck in the time when they felt they looked their best. They don't get stuck trying to duplicate a look, a haircut, clothing from an earlier time, over and over. They find it easier to remember that this body is the home for our spirit. Some may think a massage is indulgent but toxins get released in a massage; there is a benefit to sitting in a sauna; there is a benefit in simply learning to be still; there is a benefit in having quiet time whether it is a walk around the block or a week at a spa. Accepting the body in all its phases is a source of power. Television, fashion, advertising in particular are always pointing to what is wrong with our bodies, our clothes, our health, and to all the problems we should be having. The challenge is to find our own centers in the face of the pervading imagery and message. We need support groups; we need each other; we need time to ourselves to bolster what we know is true.

The portraits in this book show women who are beautifully alive in their unique physical presence and in the power centered within their deepest selves. They have been able to prune and shape the branches of their lives and become their imaginings.

The women I spoke with often shared an instinctive understanding of the body-mind connection. Some had healed themselves of serious illnesses; some were engaged in healing others. I feel that what we tell ourselves can become a self-fulfilling prophecy, that the body hears our self-talk, whether positive or negative, that holding onto old grievances and old behavior patterns that are not supportive plays into our biology and is part of what make us old.

Instead of growing old, we can grow into age, into all the different aspects of ourselves. We can grow in gratitude, in trust, in understanding of ourselves and others. We can grow in compassion. We can grow in fluidity. The media has portrayed age as rigidity, but I see age as fluidity. We have the wisdom to live in the present moment with peace, no matter what the circumstances.

I see in age the chance to grow into forgiveness, of ourselves and others, to let go of grievances and to be open to new experiences so that we do not become like root-bound plants that knurl up and turn into themselves, but like plants that get air and light and sunshine continue to unfold and to grow.

American women over sixty have in common freedoms and challenges never accorded another group in human history. We have lived through the postwar prosperity and prescriptive traditionalism of the fifties, the civil rights movement, the women's liberation movement, the counterculture and radical politics of the sixties. We came of age during the Cold War and watched the Berlin Wall come down. We traded our prom dresses for surgical masks and gowns and our dyed-silk matching heels for athletic shoes. We are the first group in world history to have had early and widespread access to reliable methods of birth control. We have been wives, mothers, same-sex partners, career women, in a variety of combinations and have constantly reinvented ourselves as we went along through marriages, divorces, budgets stretched to the core, and the joys and delights, tragedies and losses of our lives.

Research conducted by the MacArthur Foundation and reported in the book *Successful Aging* tells us that women who reach the age of sixty-five in the early twenty-first century can expect to live to eighty-four, so we will have many more opportunities to reinvent ourselves. Having left behind the stage of reproducing life, our bodies can recalibrate for the regeneration of ourselves, preparing us for a new phase that is thoughtful, liberating, fruitful. We are fully ripe with life experience and knowledge. We can be loving and kind, both to ourselves and to others. We can spread peace. We can trust and follow our intuition. I hope this book will encourage you to embrace your own life stories—and to add to them vibrant, rich chapters unrestricted by age. The world is waiting for the unique gift that you alone have to give. —GWEN MAZER, 2007

Observing We

When I began my portrait series for this book, I asked myself what it means to be working with the external manifestations of women, as we grow into the bodies of our mothers and our ancestors. How could I expose the energy, experience, and beauty of their individual identities?

I decided on black-and-white film as my medium, feeling it more poetic, more soulful, than color film. I created a consistent background to bring emphasis to my subjects' presence, one that could be used in my studio, or in their homes and conference rooms.

Historically, I looked to the inspiration of Julia Margaret Cameron for her intimate portraits of famous people, and to Edward Curtis, who immortalized our ancestors by revealing their character through clear eyes, artful wardrobe, and expressions of dignity.

As I looked at these women before my vintage field camera, I was conscious of my desire to bring out their beauty and distinction, to provide evidence that the human spirit continues for far more years in vibrancy and power than our popular culture lets on. Traces of these women's travels through time are seen in their eyes, their poise, their hands and bodies. Look closely and you will see their fortitude and fragility, the paths they have chosen and the ones that chose them—their mistakes, their accomplishments, and their humanity.

As I approach sixty, I am inspired by their willingness to show us who they are. Speaking with them, I realize that the age we are matters far less than how we live it.

The hope, the aspiration is not to be them, but, like them, to be ourselves, fully willing to ask the deep questions of who we are and what we are doing to contribute to our world. —CHRISTINE ALICINO, 2007

Wise Talk Wild Women

Had I been fortunate enough to have a math teacher with the philosophy of Marilyn Burns, I might not have been terrified by the subject. Marilyn is one of the most highly respected math educators today and the author of more than twenty books for teachers, plus a collection of math-related children's stories with titles like SPAGHETTI AND MEATBALLS FOR ALL. In 1984, she formed Marilyn Burns Education Associates, which provides training for teachers that helps them develop the abilities of children in thinking, reasoning, and problem solving through mathematics. While math is the vehicle, the goal is to encourage autonomous thought and questioning.

Marilyn Burns

Marilyn's comfortable Sausalito home is nestled among thoughtfully designed gardens that she has tended and nurtured since the 1970s. On a late fall day, we sit together in the dining area of the kitchen at an antique table with a view of the front garden. Marilyn is a woman of great wit, with a hearty laugh. Lingering traces of a Brooklyn-bred accent pepper her speech, which is frank, forthcoming, and spiced with humor.

Our conversation flows with the ease of a friendship that began when she came to me as a client more than twenty years ago. We are both New Yorkers, transplants to California, who from the moment we met realized that we shared many things in common. Looking back at her well-lived and accomplished life, I ask Marilyn what knowledge would have been valuable to her as a young woman.

"SO MANY THINGS. As you know, I came to the Bay Area in the 1960s with my husband. He had just finished medical school and was offered an internship here. We had been married about two years and I was being a wife. I wasn't being in a relationship with another human—I was playing a game. After a couple of years we divorced. By the time I was thirty I had been married and divorced twice. I was pretty shut down emotionally.

"If I had followed all the rules and hadn't started to break away little by little, I might have stayed married and raised a family, and it is unlikely that I would have gone out into the business world. That was not what I was raised to do. I was raised to teach school so that if, God forbid, I should have to work for a living, I would have the same vacation schedule as my children. The main thing then was to define yourself in terms of another person and a family. I never really wanted children, but I always thought I would have them since that was part of the plan.

"I spent so much effort as a young person trying to fit in, never letting my feelings show. Everything I did was outer-directed, everything was about pleasing my parents. I was never encouraged to trust who I was on the inside. And yet there was a kernel of something that I knew even though it wasn't valued. If I had known then that your intuition is the part of you that connects you to the universe, it would have been so much easier. I would have been more able to find a path that made sense to me. When I took oil painting classes, I could hear my mother saying, 'Enough. Now paint what I want!' I guess she wanted something she could hang on the wall. She wasn't interested in me expressing myself through art. She wasn't saying, 'What do you want to learn? Why are you so excited about painting?' She was interested in doing her job to raise me right so I could have the best chance. My piano teacher told me what to play for her recital. My choice didn't count. It wasn't worthy. A significant change came for me when I moved away from seeking the approval of others towards autonomy. It's like deciding there's no Santa Claus.

"Autonomy is what I wanted to foster in children. I wasn't interested in compliant behavior for its own sake. I wanted behavior that was intrinsically valuable for the children themselves, and that has defined my work. I don't believe in praise. Too often it's like passing judgment on a child to say 'This is behavior I like.' If a child writes a story, I might say 'Tell me why you wrote the story. How do you feel about the story? What might you do differently?' I want to find out about the child—not say to her, 'Here's what I would like to see.' Children are looking for attention and love, and what more loving thing could you say to someone than 'I am deeply interested in what you're thinking.' I'm interested in who they are, not in eliciting behavior from them that is pleasing to me. I worry that people aren't advocates for kids but are sitting on them to make them a certain way. The challenge is to work with who they are—children are so different from one another. To be successful, a relationship has to be based on respect and trust. In a relationship with a child, as opposed to one with an adult, I have a responsibility for the child's well-being, and I have to make decisions about how to exercise those responsibilities.

"My first undergraduate advisor deeply affected my work. When there was a project to do, a problem to solve, he asked you to do it in your own way. He didn't have preconceived notions about how you should do it. All my books for teachers are about teaching math in ways that work for them individually. If a teacher is comfortable teaching writing, for example, then I encourage her to use writing in math class."

I asked Marilyn about other significant changes in her life, growing in age, loss of loved ones, being in relationship, dealing with an aging parent, and finding joy and meaning in the shifting kaleidoscope of life.

"Turning forty was powerful, but turning fifty was horrifying. The number was just too big. It was half a century, and I was truly overwhelmed. At some point the power of the number faded. Now, in my sixties, I feel healthy and energetic, and over the last fifteen years I've become more physically active, with daily walks, swimming, working with a trainer, and now I'm taking yoga to help with flexibility and strength building. When I let my hair go grey, my mother and aunts just couldn't understand it. 'Grey?' said my aunt. 'You could at least go blonde.' But I love not coloring my hair. It's a wonderful kind of freedom.

"My mother was ninety-two years old when she passed, and at her ninetieth birthday she still didn't like the idea of revealing her age. She always thought of her self as 'with it,' and my father adored her. My mother said that laughter was good for your health. I think she was right. When you laugh you can't do anything else at the same time but be in the moment. Our relationship changed enormously over the years. I had spent so much of my life flying under the radar of her control, but after my father died I was the person she counted on. She was always trying to get the edge, saw manipulation and control as essential to her well-being. I think she felt that the world was not a fair place for women. Her approach to relationship was to manage it. She believed that smart women managed men—something that never made sense to me.

"I could not have imagined it earlier, but we developed a friendship, and it was surprising and interesting. I came to appreciate her spunk, her capability, honesty, complexity, and her vulnerability. She saw me as successful, secure, and accomplished, and I saw her as a little old lady without any power over my life. She would say things like 'Your father would feel better if you were married,' but she knew that I was as married as married could be, and she finally liked and accepted what she saw. She was able to let go of her fears in the end, and it was a sweet time together.

"The experiences I've had with friends and family who have died have been, in a way, wonderful gifts. My friend in Oregon chose to take her death legally when she was dying of cancer. She wanted to go out 'clean and classy,' as she put it. She wanted Frank Sinatra singing "Summer Wind," to sit in her favorite chair wearing her favorite shawl and her blue shoes. She had made a decision, and I was honored to see her through it.

"A number of years ago, I took a class in journal writing, where I learned that you could get information from within. It doesn't come from me but from this wellspring we can all dip into.

"I began to study the enneagram with Helen Palmer. She is a master in this complex system of defining and understanding personality characteristics—it has been her life work. During the years of studying with her I learned how to connect myself to the universe and work deeply with my intuition. It's what enables me to give talks and connect with people. I'm connecting with them through the universe, because we're all from the same pot. I'm not a believer in God—this is the closest I can get to defining my spiritual side. I feel wiser now because of the self examination I've done over the years. My current practice is learning how to be present and completely open in the moment. Whether I am reading a book, gardening, teaching, or sitting and talking with a friend, I want to be in that moment fully.

"I am slowing down my pace, looking forward to time in my garden, having less stress, spending more time with my life partner. We have been together for a third of my life. During the first twelve years of our relationship, we commuted, as his obligations were on the East Coast. When he retired and it was possible for us to live together I was wary of the idea. I wasn't sure I could handle the intimacy. We each had our own lives, lots of hellos, and glorious romance. But it has been wonderful. He has three daughters and eight grandchildren. They are now part of my world, and I have learned how to be giving and supportive in another way.

"Being in a relationship has softened me and keeps me soft because you have to give to get and you have to be present. When I was younger, even though I might be in a relationship, I could be steely from the outside and very much alone. I used to say, 'A woman needs a man like a fish needs a bicycle.' But to have a partner, male or female, to have the caring and intimacy, the being held, the being touched, it makes the years richer and warmer. To have good friends, connection—that adds to our pleasure and joy and becomes even more meaningful as we grow in age."

At ninety-eight, artist Frances Dunham Catlett seems to have more energy and interests than many women half her age. This striking African American woman with her crown of white hair moves with the ease and grace of a dancer, crackles with humor, and has an ageless sense of the possibilities life offers. On a summer afternoon we sit in her studio home in Berkeley, California, with the view of a magnolia tree spilling lush blossoms and a sky tumbled with fluffy white clouds. One part of her studio is packed with paintings. On an adjacent wall are photographs of her family, shelves of books, scrapbooks from her world travels—a thick montage of memorabilia.

Frances Dunham Catlett

As the youngest of ten siblings, Frances is the last living member of her family's post-slavery generation and the repository of its history. Recently I attended the opening of her one-woman show, THE GIFT OF COLOR, *at a prominent northern California gallery. The place was packed with collectors and friends. With over fifty museum and gallery exhibitions since her first show in the early 1960s, she has continued the artistic tradition of a family that includes poets, musicians, fine artists, and educators.*

"IT WAS NOT MY INTENTION to become an artist—my sisters Ida and Rebecca were the designated artists in the family. Ida liked to work with found materials—she wrote a book on the subject as a guide for teachers—and Rebecca liked to paint what she saw. She married the first bishop of the Virgin Islands and belonged to an art club there but never made a living from art. We used to tease each other because I liked to paint what I felt—for me it was a way of exploring the mystery of the universe.

"I really didn't know I had any artistic talent until the 1950s. I had a secret plan to be a dancer (after I finished college and could support myself), even though I was growing up in a church that taught that dancing was a sin. Years later a group of my friends—we were all social workers—invited me to join them for art classes at the De Young Museum in San Francisco, and I loved it. Once I retired from social work I was able to focus completely on my art. I continued at the Art Institute. I studied with a great teacher there, a colorist, who really encouraged me—and it all just dropped into my hands.

"I completed my master's in art at Mills College in Oakland—I was the first African American to graduate there. During this time I also started doing hatha yoga. Once you learn it you always have the exercises you can do. With my friend, who was also one of my art teachers, I was learning classical guitar, something I keep saying I want to practice again, but there never seems to be enough time to do all the things I enjoy!"

Being with Frances Catlett is a great reminder that many aspects of age have to do with your state of mind, ability to evolve and change, to let things go and begin again. She has always followed her internal muse, having faith in where the journey might take her. More than sixteen years ago she had colon cancer and never skipped a beat. Now in her late nineties, she plays a weekly four- to five-hour game of Scrabble with friends. It keeps the mind agile, she says. She bowls twice a week with two leagues. She plays bridge with a group that has been getting together for over twenty years. She loves sports and keeps up with baseball, golf, and tennis.

Frances was born in Hartford, Connecticut. Her parents had come north from Virginia in the late 1800s. Her father and two others founded Hartford's Union Baptist Church, still in operation today in a building nominated for the National Register of Historic Places.

"My father worked, was a minister, and was active in the community. My mother stayed home to take care of us. She had an expression: 'Make it do, do without it, mend it, fix it.' She was a seamstress and remade everything for each child, so when I got a brand-new dress all my own I thought that was something.

"I was a very lonesome person, as I was the youngest and could never catch up with my sisters, but on Sunday afternoons we would all get together and have a great time. My sister Rebecca played the piano, and we would sing all afternoon. Our house had two lots, one for the house and one for the garden. We had all kinds of fruit trees, and a lawn surrounding the house with flowers and space to play croquet and other games. My mother knew everything in the forest that was good to eat, and she canned everything from the garden. My father went to the market only to get meat. Remember that when I was a child there were no cars—the iceman and the vegetable man came by in their horse-drawn carts.

"While we lived in a predominantly white neighborhood, there were several black families. The strength and stability of my family was a major factor in my life. The few times that I was called names I would repeat the rhyme about 'Sticks and Stones,' or my sisters would come to my defense, but for the most part it was pretty peaceful. Our family took advantage of everything that was available to us, good schools, the library. We were expected to excel in school and we did. I tied academically all through school with another girl for the best grades, and a scholarship was available to college for whoever won. A black family set up a scholarship for any black student in the city of Hartford with the highest grades, and I won. I chose to go to the University of Chicago because my sister lived in Chicago, and they had an excellent arts program there.

"I was still so innocent when I went to college I thought that if somebody kissed you, you might become pregnant. At that time we were taught by religion that sex was a lower thing and not that important. I played tennis with a very nice fellow who used to carry my books and walk me home. He was very proper. I don't know what I would have done if he had made a pass at me. When I got my menstrual period the only instruction I got from my mother was to keep my skirts down, and I didn't understand what she meant by that.

"When I arrived at the University of Chicago and went to the dorm, the staircases had all of these incredible Oriental rugs flung over the railings, and that was the beginning of the end of my provincialism. My friend knew a man who had some time, and she asked him to show me the city. He was a very nice guy who later wanted to marry me. He took me everywhere, including this place that had a sign outside that read 'Leave Your Innocence Outside,' and this was where I heard one of the entertainers say the word 'penis,' a word I had never said in my whole life—what a waking-up I got.

"So much creativity was all around me. Artists, writers, and poets who were part of the Harlem Renaissance were coming from New York, someone started a play group, everything was so intellectually stimulating, and I got into thick of it. I was going to classes all day, then we would practice theatre, and from there we would go dancing. I would stumble home at about 7 o'clock and have an 8 o'clock class. My sister would tease me and threaten to write home to my parents. I took ballet classes and I went to every modern dance concert there was, Martha Graham, Nijinski, Isadora Duncan and her brother."

Among the most respected members of Frances's group of friends at the university was Albert Dunham, a philosopher, a man of intellectual brilliance, and the brother of Frances's roommate Katherine Dunham, who later became world renown as a dancer. Frances and Albert fell in love, were married, and moved to Boston, where Albert had received a fellowship at Harvard.

Frances completed her studies and graduated from Boston University. Her husband took a position at Howard University teaching philosophy, and she was able to study modern dance with a teacher who came from New York. Her husband was emotionally fragile and ultimately succumbed to severe mental illness. During this period her first son was born.

"Albert was the love of my life, my soulmate, and it was writing poetry that got me through the next five years of living without him. When I look back, I regret that I understood so little about psychiatry and psychology. He was being seen by some of the great minds of the time, and I thought he was in good hands.

"After becoming a wife and mother, I had to find a job, and my career as a social worker began. One of the popular theories about raising babies at the time was that it was not good to hold them or pick them up too much, something that went completely against my instincts. To this day I have regrets that I followed the books of the time instead of my feelings.

"I married twice after Albert. Each husband was very brilliant—my sister said 'Fran, can't you just find an ordinary man?' I was hoping for a wonderful father for my son but when I had a son by my second husband it was clear that children were not very interesting to him. He died of a perforated ulcer. I had also known his family before we married. They were wonderful people, his sister was the sculptor Elizabeth Catlett."

Frances Catlett has experienced two world wars, the invention of talking movies, television, the computer and the internet, the advent of women's suffrage, the civil rights movement, the women's movement, and the movement toward women becoming single mothers by choice, with no stigma attached.

During her years as a social worker she developed an innovative program for girls who became pregnant out of wedlock and were sent away in disgrace to have their children. We talked about world events, responsibility, young people, and I asked if she felt a sense of peace.

"I am truly disturbed by many things that are happening. I have to stop my head from thinking about what's going on in this world because that does not give me any peace. I hate to say it, but it seems to me when I simply get up in the morning and go to a bowling alley and I don't have to answer all the questions the world is asking me and I can just use my body to throw a ball, I'm comfortable. When I listen to classical music and hear something that I have loved for a long time, and I can just lie there and listen, it's peaceful. I look out at the trees and remember how strong their trunks are and how they just stand there and wait. They don't fight. They seem to be at peace just to be what they are.

"Gatherings of people give me delight, gatherings of people I have known for a long time—you don't have to explain you to them, and they don't have to explain them to you. It's this sense of life that you give each other. I think of my ninety-seventh picnic birthday out in the green with all of these wonderful friends. I could come home to these empty rooms and feel abandoned, but I have all this to sustain me. I am not religious but I am a spiritual person. It is the experience of what is not obvious that hits you in the heart when you don't expect it and somehow gives you a deeper understanding of life. I don't believe in afterlife. My theory is that the universe is kept going by me after I die. I'm part of the food of the universe and it will take from me whatever it needs."

Frances Catlett has drunk fully from the cup of life and continues to do so. In so doing she may have found one of the golden keys to an ageless, timeless life.

"I STARTED WORKING AT FOURTEEN, and my childhood was chaotic, going back and forth between my parents and aunt. I didn't grow up with parents who could be guides. When I went to high school in Berkeley, California, in the early 1950s there were about 2,000 students there and only about 200 were black. After high school, I was the only one in my group of friends who didn't head off to college—I was accepted to San Francisco State but there was no money for me to go. It was a very lonely time. I married the boy next door, and, like everyone at that time, I had children. After a difficult marriage and a terrible divorce I was a single mother of two. I was working for the Navy and doing volunteer work for the March of Dimes and the NAACP.

Belva Davis

"Then I got a fragment of information from a couple of photographers who were talking about the problem of supplying copy to go with photographs they were sending to the magazine they were working for. It was Johnson Publications, the leading black publication at the time. I found out who to talk to, called the person up, and got a job as an unpaid stringer for *Jet Magazine.*

"This was the beginning, the first step toward a career in journalism, radio, and eventually television. As I had no experience or background I would simply conceive an idea, try to find out as much as I could, proceed to try to do it, and if it didn't work, come up with another plan.

"There had been a long period in my life that felt like sleepwalking—I had cocooned myself with books and films. When I woke up, I was ravenous for life and full of curiosity. This was the beginning of my taking risks, and it's how I began to create a new life for myself.

"If I could say anything about my life, it is one that has been lived on intuition and in trust of that intuition."

Nob Hill, San Francisco, California. I am at the home of Belva Davis, and the phone is ringing off the hook. Calls come constantly. She unplugs the phone but it still rings in another room. We are in her sunshine-yellow dining room, its floor-to-ceiling windows draped in golden silk taffeta that puddles to the floor. As the first African American woman hired to work in television in the western United States, Belva has been cooking on all four burners for over forty years and is one of the most honored and respected journalists in the business.

A small-boned woman with an air of grace, an engaging smile, and fierce determination who earned her reputation through trial by fire, she says that she is still very shy. At the time we spoke, she insisted that she was trying to move at a slower pace, and she was winding down her position as president of the board of directors of the new Museum of the African Diaspora, for which she spearheaded the capital campaign. She continues hosting her weekly show "This Week in Northern California" on PBS station KQED, which received the 2004 Crystal Award of Excellence for its public affairs coverage, and she continues working on a variety of community projects and serving on several boards. She has always been committed to supporting African American culture and history.

For over forty years, Belva has been married to William Moore, whom she calls her best friend. They have shared a lifetime of adventures and parallel groundbreaking careers, his as the first African American television news cameraman.

At last the phones stop ringing, the momentary crises are handled, and we settle in at the dining table to talk.

"Eventually I got a job writing for two black news publications, the *Bay Area Independent* and the *Sun Reporter,* and with the help of some of the more seasoned men in the business began to get a handle on what I was doing. I was also focused on a career in radio and got my first job at KSAN basically collecting and reading news clips on the air. I used to practice with a tape recorder, reading in front of a mirror to remember to get my facial expression to match my voice tone.

"I was single again, and for the first time I was just having fun. Warner Brothers had sold one of its stations, and it became the local black radio station KDIA. My next job was at the station, at first handling the traffic for the spots the salesmen sold.

"I was dying of curiosity about people, everything, and my news director, Lou Freeman, had an international view of the world. He took me to the National Republican Convention in 1964—this was a pivotal moment in my political awakening. He also exposed me to people like Gunnar Myrdal, the great Swedish economist who won a Nobel Prize for his work. I had to read his book so that I was prepared to interview him when he came to our station, and this was a real introduction into how other societies think.

"KDIA was the station that spoke to the black population, so I interviewed Martin Luther King, Malcolm X, and many others. Finally I got my own show as a disc jockey on Saturday afternoons playing a variety of music, including a lot of jazz. Bill was really knowledgeable and chose a lot of the music. We also got married during this time, and I went from a bad marriage to a good marriage—one that I was happy and perfectly satisfied with.

"The station was set up in the old Warner Brothers studios that were a series of log cabins and cottages. I would invite different musicians and personalities who were appearing at the Jazz Workshop, Enrico's, and the Hungry I to the station for interviews. Everyone came—from Bill Cosby and Horace Silver to Mel Torme and Nancy Wilson. My sponsors were Foster Farms Chicken, Wonder Bread, Coke, Pepsi, Del Monte Cling Peaches, and Best Foods Sandwich Spread. So I decided that a great way to boost my ratings was to host these Saturday lunches and invite the radio audience. Well, this became a huge family project. I was at home frying chicken, making peach cobbler and potato salad. At the studio Bill manned the buffet table, my son greeted the guests, and my daughter, who was still a little toddler, just had fun. It was really crazy, but a lot of famous people would drop by. You never knew who would just show up.

"Our life just evolved that way, and the children were always part of it. We both had unpredictable schedules, so eventually we had a nanny. She would give the children an early dinner snack and when we came home late in the evening we would all sit down to a family dinner. They loved it. Recently my daughter Darolyn said that when they were kids it was hard to focus on school because life at home was so interesting. She recalled coming home from school one day to find Horace Silver playing the piano and Alex Haley signing a copy of his book *Roots*. Then the doorbell rang and Ron Dellums stopped in.

"Up to this point all my experience had been in segregated markets. I began to realize that the real future in media was television and set myself the goal of becoming a part of it. Television news reporting was just evolving, and news was expanding from fifteen minutes to half an hour at night. I heard that Nancy Reynolds at KPIX was leaving to become press secretary at the White House, and I decided to apply for the job. Ultimately there were sixty-seven candidates.

"When I was hired—after many interviews and losing ten pounds—I was the first black woman to work on television west of the Mississippi. As a person who had one of the first jobs, I felt a great sense of responsibility to do well and, in a way, the burden, mixed with the opportunity, to dispel some of the myths about people that looked like me, and I took that whole effort personally to heart. Bill and I realized that this was a big step, and, realizing that, Bill stayed home and took care of the children so that I could concentrate totally on trying to build this career. So Bill became a house husband early on and had a ball—we all did that first year.

"The station didn't want me to be pigeonholed but the civil rights movement was underway, as well as movements with the Black Panthers, Malcolm X, the Black Muslims, and the free speech movement at Berkeley. With my peer group, I was just another reporter who was supposed to approach a story as any other reporter. I concentrated on making sure that I covered a variety of communities, people, and events without neglecting the community I represented. My advantage was that I knew some of the people involved in these movements from prior associations, and sometimes they sought me out. We all had to have the ability to cover the world from some medium point.

"During this time Bill and I began to work on the idea of him getting into the photographers' union, which he was able to do, and a year or so later he went to work for KTVU."

Our conversation turns to age. Since television is known for ending the careers of most woman at thirty-five, I ask Belva how she had negotiated a career that was not affected by her age.

"I never hid or lied about my age, just dealt with where I was in my work life. I tried to stay ahead of the game by going in before anyone asked me to leave and saying 'I want to do something else,' and finding something to do that I was comfortable with. I have been able, thank God, to make accommodations with myself. When I wanted to show a different, softer side and became the spokesperson for the Season of Sharing program that raises money for the needy at Christmas, I could let go of the persona of the hard news reporter. I'm fortunate to have a partner who, whatever decision I make—whether it's lead anchoring or doing something else—is there for support."

We speak about what a wonderful gift it is to have a life partner who has championed her and reflected her in the best light. She laughs and says, "Isn't he a genius!"

"Bill has been the steadying person. I know that ours is a true partnership, and I'm only beginning to know how valuable that is as we are in our seventies. Every single day when we have dinner the conversation is so full. We laugh a lot. We can discuss events from different points of view. The view of the reporter is vastly different from that of the cameraman. He's at the steps of Air Force One as it lands and I'm somewhere further back with the reporters.

"Life has been so amazing. We read an article in the newspaper the other day about one of the maître d's at the Fairmont and remembered how we used to go on media night to the Venetian Room in the hotel for dinner, dancing, and a show. We saw everybody—Lena Horne, Nat King Cole, Bing Crosby.

"In a way, I wish that I had been more observant of my own life. I often felt I was just twirling from one incredible moment to the next, so much to learn from the amazing people I met through the interview desk, presidents, governors, scientists. I would be enthralled, and then the next thing would happen. One of the most thrilling moments, and I think this is true for every reporter, was the first time reporting from the White House lawn.

"There was a time in my life when I felt this kind of loneliness that comes with age, when you realize how many of your friends are gone. Losing your parents makes you stand up and look—becoming the senior person in your family calls you to attention. You begin to realize that there's a shorter time on the end.

"I am a deeply spiritual person. I do not follow any religious doctrine, but I talk with God every day. I hope in my heart that when things are not going my way I am able to withstand the consequences, rather than to pray for the outcome I want. Bill and I get up on Sunday and say 'Where shall we go to church today?' We do this whether we are traveling or at home. I think it is the least I can do, to offer one hour of my week to sitting and seeing what comes from opening up to the experience, and I hope it helps me build on my internal beliefs."

Belva's children have been an integral part of her career, sharing many adventures with her as she covered various assignments. I ask what she learned from raising them.

"Children have their own chemistry, and it's very difficult for parents to accept that. You try to mold and shape, but they come to you with ingrained characteristics. You can only do so much, and you can't ruin a child's life or yours by trying to superimpose what you think is right upon them. That's the hard, hard lesson in parenting. It's the accommodation that we both end up having to make with each other. They were far too sophisticated and grown up for their age, and I finally realized that I had created the circumstances for that to happen. One of the joys in my life is the wonderful relationship I have with my children now. They call every morning. They say that I have slowed down enough for them to become more attentive."

With a thread of information, determination to develop skills, wonderful mentors along the way, and the deep voice of her intuition, Belva has woven the magic for her own life.

There is a flow to each of our lives, and recognizing its rhythm may be one of the secrets to finding the path of seemingly effortless unfolding.

Donna Eden's presence is like sunshine. She envelops you with a glow that seems to come from her very being. As one of the foremost practitioners and teachers of energy medicine, she embodies her healing work.

Donna Eden

Her practice has its roots in healing traditions thousands of years old that are being reinterpreted and understood more clearly today. We all have subtle energy systems, pathways that affect our health and well-being, the more familiar ones being our meridians, chakras, and aura. She has the unusual ability to see and interpret the movement, colors, and patterns of the anatomy of subtle energy and has developed practices that can bring these energies into balance and health. As we were introduced, her first comment was about the swirling purple-violet color she saw emanating from and surrounding my body.

Donna's book ENERGY MEDICINE is highly respected as one of the most definitive interpretations of a subject that is moving rapidly into the mainstream of health and healing. I spent an evening at one of her filled-to-overflowing seminars, where she explained and demonstrated the use of applied kinesiology, a form of muscle testing, body movements, and exercises to change the flow of energy. She presented amazingly simple methods for healing yourself of headaches and colds, releasing anger, stress, and exhaustion, and becoming more aware, enlivened, and focused. With her husband of twenty-one years, clinical psychologist David Feinstein, she travels around the world giving lectures, attending conferences, and training in ways to work with much more serious illness.

"I WAS TWENTY-ONE YEARS OLD before I found out the whole world didn't see energy—it was one of the biggest shocks of my life as it was so natural to me and so much a part of my upbringing. My mother always saw energy, and she gave that to us as children. From the time I was very little she'd say, 'Do you see that color coming out of that person? What do you see? Are we seeing the same thing?' It was just part of conversation.

"I'm convinced that most babies are born able to see energy but because the ability is not kept alive in our culture, it just goes dormant. When I was living in Fiji, I found that most children there who lived in the natural environment saw energy—it was part of the rhythms and cycles of the earth. For the ones who lived in the city, it was a mixed bag.

"I grew up in the mountains of Ramona, California, in a very loving family. I think I was very lucky because I was the middle child and got to slide through without too much attention on me. My sister was the first-born—she was extremely beautiful— my brother, who was born shortly after me, was gorgeous, and I was kind of cute. My mother used to say, 'Oh, Donna, you're the lucky one. Your sister is going to have to deal with people seeing her beauty and not getting beyond that, but you, you're able to develop from the inside without anybody judging what you look like.' And I did think that was the better way. There was no fear placed in me, where my sister had a lot of fear—to not do this or that because boys will do this and that.

"I've read all the articles about the middle child, but for me it was terrific. I felt loved and trusted. When I was little, my mother became very ill with tuberculosis and was expected to die. She refused to stay on medication and we were quarantined at home. She got well by eating naturally, growing everything in the backyard and taking vitamin C. She became very sick again when I was a teenager and again she was able to heal herself. From childhood I suffered a variety of illnesses, including tuberculosis, and struggled with severe PMS from the age of twelve. So, early on I was exposed to the ways that the body can heal itself.

"My first husband threatened to have me put in a mental institution if I ever talked about seeing energy—he was paralyzed with fear that people would think he was married to a nut case. So I tried not to see or make decisions by energy, and that was the loneliest time of my life. My health got worse and worse because I was not living true to myself. Boy, I really can understand a woman who can't leave a man who beats her. While I was never physically beaten—it was more psychological—my spirit and will were so beaten down that it took everything I had to lift myself out.

"Marrying into that family was hard. They were so different from anything I knew. They were a prominent underworld family. Somehow, when I first saw him from a distance I knew that he would be the father of my children, and I had two daughters with him. But I did not want my daughters to grow up in this environment, to have their spirits broken and be married off into that structure. There were threats of having my children taken away from me, and it took everything I had to leave that marriage. I had become so ill my organs were breaking down, but I was able to heal myself before I got out. I wanted to live because I could not imagine someone in that environment raising my girls.

"When I was diagnosed with symptoms of multiple sclerosis, I started to heal myself with energy techniques. I never thought I would be able to do this with others— this was in the 1970s, and I knew someone who had been jailed for doing something only close to what I did. I walked away with my two kids holding onto my legs, half a jar of peanut butter, and less than one dollar. When I walked out the door I felt freedom. I knew that everything would be okay, it was like angels carried us on wings.

"All my adult years I've heard women say, when they get a divorce or have to go out on their own, 'Well, thank goodness, at least I don't have children.' But I loved being on my own and raising my daughters. I found that having children gave me the strength and courage to do things I never thought I could do, and the only thing I could really do is my work. Without them I might have thought that I had to be a secretary or something else I wasn't good at.

"What I know about the body is an absolute—it wants to heal itself. Auto-immune illnesses are the body gone berserk trying to figure out how to do that. There is too much to deal with, too much energy coming in from what is unnatural, stresses that we didn't evolve to live with, and so the body starts attacking us. If you can get on the same wavelength as your energy systems, which are incredibly intelligent—far more intelligent than your intellect—they will know how to heal you, but you have to get into alignment. After I healed myself, I began to work with others who had multiple sclerosis, and every one of them got well. I had started doing massage and somehow people had just started to show up."

Donna continued to elaborate on the turns of her life, which led to me ask about the most adventuresome things she had done. She described her experience living in Fiji and how it further opened the doorway into what she does today.

"A number of years after I left my husband, whom I had not legally divorced, he invited the girls and me to travel with him to the South Seas, as he needed to complete his dissertation for his Ph.D. and wanted to spend some time with the children. I was a lot stronger, so I agreed, and we went off to Fiji. He had worked very hard to escape his background. I saw the goodness in him that had first attracted me, and we were able to complete our relationship.

"He returned to the States, and I stayed on with my children for two years in Fiji and Tahiti—spearing fish, eating everything that was natural and fresh.

"During that time, I was bitten by a deadly insect and became very sick. The local shamans heard what had happened and came with a treatment for the bite. They dug a hole in the sand and buried me there, with just my head sticking out, for long periods of time over several days. They believed that the toxins would be drained into the sand. I felt they knew what they were doing. It was as if I had come home to something I understood. I wanted to work with them, to learn, and they gave me language for what I just knew.

"On several of the islands, every woman had five days a month coinciding with her menstrual period to call her own. Even if she worked in the two major cities of Fiji, in schools or government offices, a woman was able to retreat to her own moon hut. They believed that this was the most powerful time of a women's life, so every woman left her home, and other women would take care of her children so she could be alone. At times, on the third day a tribal leader might ask her to review a big decision while she was in this time of depth, and she would come back and give him a message. Young girls were thrilled when their time came. They could do as they wished, invite father, grandmother, or the spirit of their ancestors into the hut to ask them question about life."

I was moved by this story of a place where for five days each month a woman is a goddess. How different from the western idea of having "the monthly curse." I imagined how such thinking might give young western men and women a new way of relating to their bodies and to each other, and I wondered if it would make a difference in sexual abuse.

I mentioned to Donna that I had read a newspaper article about how full-bodied young women in Fiji who were being exposed to television for the first time were becoming ashamed of their bodies and were trying to diet.

"When I returned to the States after being away for almost two years, I was in such culture shock. I hadn't been in a car, seen a newspaper, or used a phone, radio, or television for all that time, and had eaten only pure foods. Back in the States I could taste what my food had been packaged in, the cardboard, the lining, my sense of taste was so clear.

"Shortly after my return, we moved to a rural little town because I didn't want to raise the girls in a city. I went to see this woman doctor who was well recommended and mentioned that I was going to have to figure out how to have a moon hut there. She took my hand and said, 'Donna, I just want to give you some friendly advice. Don't ever talk about that again, dear. We can't have that. Women want to be able to run for president so we can't have that kind of thing. We've got to act more like men here.'

"In the airport the day of my return I saw a woman wearing a T-shirt that said 'Touch For Health,' and she said, 'I'm so excited, I'm going to be a Touch for Health instructor.' And I heard myself say, 'Me too'—and that's how I found John Thie's organization, started the training, and learned energy testing and other techniques. His belief that you can give people tools to heal themselves formed the basis of some of the practices that I use."

We talked about women's attitudes toward age, relationships, sensuality, and what would have been useful for us to know as younger women. She laughed at that last question.

"It would have been useful to know how glorious it is to be in your sixties! When I grew up it was 'Don't trust anyone over thirty.' Each decade has gotten better. Life gets clearer in your soul and psyche. Things that I thought were mistakes were not mistakes at all. When you realize that nobody has it all down, you are less intimidated. I did have a sense of aging in my late forties, and it was because of the media, but I snapped out of it.

"I have been working on women's bodies a long time and have found that when we hit our early fifties we either get better or worse. I've seen it over and over—it has a lot to do with this belief in age, accepting the idea that we aren't vital, sexy, or attractive, which is ludicrous.

"Who knows what years I look like. I don't dress to my age. I feel more empowered, authentic, sexy, and natural than ever. As I look into my future, I have more appreciation for the cycles of human life we are graced to go through.

"I don't want be younger or to pretend to be different than I am. The gift is to go full measure all the way."

When I asked Donna about her spiritual beliefs, she grinned and clapped her hands.

"Oh terrific, I get to tell you my story.

"I have always had a sense of coming from another place. My first memory is of being about two months old, lying in my crib, remembering where I came from, and feeling connected to that place and loving that I could go back and remember it every day. My mother comes in—she is wearing a dress with red flowers—and my father comes and puts his arm around her and together they're oohing and aahing at me in my crib. And I am thinking, I'm so much older than they are but I am in this little body and they don't know that I'm older than they are! This was my first conscious thought.

"Much of my life feels like learning how to be here on planet Earth. I have always felt I was a very old soul but not one that had been on Earth a lot. One of my strongest memories from when I was three or four years old is sitting and talking with a giant angel.

"I meditate every day. David and I also do something once or twice a week where our entire evening is spent listening within and then talking about it. That has always been a big part of our journey together."

I asked Donna what brought particular joy to her life.

"One of the major things that brings me joy is seeing people step into their soul's journey not afraid to be who they were meant to be. I've seen both my kids doing that, and it just blows me away. I love knowing that I have left people with some tools to empower and heal themselves and their families. I love giving children techniques for moving their own energy so that they can learn better and not feel stupid. That is a very important part of my journey and my work.

"Right now I am excited and intellectually challenged, as I'm writing a book on the energy of women's hormones, what to do through menopause, so that women can have another way to work energetically and heal themselves."

Well-practiced in the art of ikebana, the formal tea ceremony, calligraphy, and playing the shamsien, Keiko Fukuda is a study in contrasts. She is the highest ranking woman in the world in judo, the Japanese martial art. She is the only one to hold double red belts, the first and only woman to be honored with this distinguished award from the Kodokan Judo Institute in Japan and the United States Judo Federation. She performed in the Olympics in Tokyo in 1964 and for more than seventy years has traveled the world teaching and training.

Sensei Keiko Fukuda

Recently, the Schlesinger Library at Radcliffe became the repository for Keiko's archives so they are available for students to study. She is a National Living Treasure in Japan and has received the Order of the Sacred Treasure, Gold Rays with Rosette, and numerous other awards. At the age of ninety-two she is still able to throw her opponents and students on the mat.

I met Sensei Fukuda, accompanied by her dear friend and companion of over forty years, Dr. Shelley Fernandez, at the dojo for women, the Soko Joshi Judo Club in San Francisco, that Keiko established in 1973. Although she is less than five feet tall, you can feel the fierce "ju" energy she is capable of conjuring up in an instant. While she walks with a cane, has had triple bypass surgery, and must sit during most of the class, she focuses closely on her students' every move, at times getting up to demonstrate the detail of a technique.

Students at the dojo range in age, the youngest being girls of thirteen, and they come from every walk of life. They include the first woman conductor of the San Francisco Opera as well as doctors and lawyers, and some have studied with Keiko for many years. Some travel regularly to be with her; others have actually relocated to be nearby.

This gentle, soft-spoken woman, whose motto is 'Be strong, be gentle, be beautiful,' is the last living student of the founder of judo, Jigoro Kano Shihan. Kano was a student of her grandfather, Hachinosuke Fukuda, a famous Ju-Jitsu samurai.

So how did a young woman from a traditional Japanese family of the early twentieth century manage to break the rules and carve out such an unusual life for herself, when it was expected that, like every upper-class Japanese woman, she would marry and move into the home of her husband's family?

Japanese is still Sensei Fukuda's first language, so I speak with her with the assistance of Shelley Fernandez in order to learn her unusual story.

"DURING THE FESTIVITIES for the fiftieth anniversary of the Kokodan Judo School I met Kano Shihan, and shortly thereafter he came to our home for tea. During his visit he told us that the Kodokan now had a Women's Division and encouraged me to come. I had finished my degree in Japanese literature at Shoa University so I went with my mother to visit the school.

"I had never seen anything like these movements before, and I was fascinated. Although my uncle objected, the next year I enrolled in the classes. Training was every day from three to six in the evening, the time that all married women are overseeing and preparing for their husband's dinner. So only unmarried women could take the class. That is still the tradition today."

It was about 1935 when Keiko Fukuda began her classes. While she was studying, her mother enlisted the services of a marriage maker. A suitable husband was found, a man who was also a student of judo, and Keiko agreed to the marriage—until she was told that once married she would no longer be able to continue her studies. At this point she was an assistant teacher and had become immersed in judo, feeling that she was guided by the spirit of her grandfather. She refused the marriage arrangement, something that it was highly unusual to do. As both her father and her grandfather were dead, there were no men who could force her to marry.

At the time of her father's death, her brother had received the family inheritance, since women were not allowed to inherit. So Keiko lived in the family home with her mother, her brother, and his family. Her mother became ill, and it was Keiko's responsibility to care for her. She continued teaching judo, for which she was paid thirty-five dollars a month— strictly used to cover her train fare to and from the school. The responsibility for her well-being belonged to her brother, according to tradition.

"I went to a fortune teller to speak with her about my mother's illness. They sit on the streets at night, illuminated by lanterns, and it is the custom to consult with them. She told me that if I would change my name I would be famous one day, and that I would travel to distant lands doing judo. She gave me the name of Keiko. After that I asked everyone to call me by that name, but my mother never could.

"All during the war I went to the kodokan and taught judo. There were fires everywhere from the bombings, and our family lost twenty of our houses, all but one. In the 1950s, a woman came from America to study at the school, and she enjoyed my teaching. With her influence, I was sponsored by the Northern California Judo Association to teach in the United States. Ten years later, when I was in my fifties, through another American, I came to the United States again. By this time I had been to Australia to teach and had competed in the Olympics in Tokyo.

"I was touring and teaching judo in California, and through one of my students I met Dr. Fernandez, who became an enthusiastic student. She was a graduate of Mills College and arranged for us to do a demonstration there with some of my Samoan students, very big men. This is how I was offered a position to teach judo at Mills. I had my ticket to go back to Japan, but Shelley invited me to stay at her home so I had a place to live. This was the first time I earned my own money."

This invitation turned into a life of adventure for Sensei Fukuda and for Dr. Fernandez, who acted as translator as the two traveled the world together. Keiko taught and demonstrated judo in the Philippines, Ireland, Mexico, Norway, Canada, Israel, Australia, even in the Antarctic, where they had never seen an Asian person before. She eventually became an American citizen and never left the home of her friend.

A small apartment of Dr. Fernandez's building became Keiko's first judo studio and over the years housed many visiting students, including a young Frenchman who came under Keiko's tutelage and studied with her for four years. He returned to France to start a judo school, where her picture hangs in honor.

Years later, he invited her there to teach a group of black belt male judo teachers who came from all over France for the occasion. When they met this tiny woman they were furious. They didn't want a woman teacher, and certainly not one who was eighty years old. But when she started demonstrating and they realized that she was truly a master, everything changed. They brought her back to France a second time and invited the mayor of Paris to her demonstration, and he in turn arranged a grand ceremony and honored her with a medal.

Keiko has written two important books on judo, one just released. On the rare occasions when she isn't traveling and can relax at home, she loves shopping for and cooking all the traditional meals she was trained to prepare, answering by hand the international correspondence she receives, enjoying her cat, which she taught to fetch, and dining in her favorite French restaurant. "When I am old, I will slow down," she says.

Every New Year, Sensei Fukuda holds a celebration, feast, and traditional ceremony of respect, the Kagami Biraki, in honor of her mentor, the founder of the Kodokan, and to acknowledge the spiritual aspects of the practice of judo. Demonstrations showcase the accomplishments of the students for the year, and sensei from all over the world attend.

I asked her what have been the rewards of her career. She mentioned gaining respect for her knowledge, especially from men in Japan (where she was finally awarded the highest honor, one that had long been denied her because she was a woman). She also takes joy in the living the legacy of her students, the opportunity to travel all over the world, and in the richness of living with the guiding spiritual principles of her art and the spirit of her grandfather, who is always with her and who is happy she chose judo as her destiny.

At the time of our meeting, Nikki Giovanni was in the throes of loss and grief. In the space of several months, she had lost both her mother and her sister to cancer. She was at a question mark. Who was she, now that she was no longer a daughter or a sister? She said her mother was her audience, that she wanted to be famous for her, and now she would have to recreate herself, and a community, for this new time in her life. For a great poet, painful questioning and the reframing of identity will inevitably weave its way into language. Nikki's latest book, ACOLYTES, is a tribute to her mother.

Nikki Giovanni

I met Nikki in the early 1970s, during the days of the civil rights movement, when she was a young mother, rebellious activist, and poet, and I interviewed her for my "Lifestyle" pages in HARPER'S BAZAAR. Over the years she has produced an immense body of work and become one of America's most widely read poets as well as a distinguished professor at Virginia Polytechnic Institute in Blacksburg, and is the recipient of many honorary doctorates. We met in San Francisco, where she was stopping on a book tour for her latest children's book, the story of Rosa Parks, and to attend the prestigious Caldecott dinner that celebrates excellence in children's book illustration. Bryan Collier, the illustrator of Nikki's book ROSA, won Caldecott honors for his illustrations for the book. ROSA also won the Coretta Scott King Award.

Nikki is a great cook, having learned the finer points of southern cooking from the women in her family, and in our conversation was puzzling over the missing ingredient in

a recipe of her mother's she had recently made. "I think I forgot the bay leaves," she said as we traded recipes and stories. San Francisco holds fond memories for her, from times she shared there with her mother enjoying the city's great cuisine, so we spent some time in restaurants she loved or wanted to experience. Nikki both loved and liked her mother. Her mother played jazz piano and they loved listening to jazz together. Deeply grieving the loss of beloved family members, and rooted in many ways to southern tradition, Nikki was thinking about the meaning of family, friends, motherhood, and shared DNA.

"I THINK FAMILIES WORK when everybody recognizes the family as a business. Maybe it's an accident of DNA, birth, and legalities, but however we come together, it's still a business. It has a CEO, and everyone has a job to do. People need to step up when Grandmother dies, Mother steps up, the oldest daughter steps up, everybody steps up to do the jobs that have to be done. In my opinion, it's crazy in this country right now that people don't say, 'What am I doing for the family?' Instead it's 'What is the family doing for me?'

"At a certain point it was important to move my mother, sister, and aunts to live near me. We could comfort each other, but we all needed our space—they needed their home and I needed mine, and I could make that happen. Growing up in a poor home, the only time I had had my own bedroom was when I lived with my grandmother, so it's very nice to have my everything, and I wasn't giving that up!

"I took on my mother's friends, the widows and the divorcees, because that's what you do as you get older. They were constantly together and shared family meals. Why should they be alone? One of them, whom I dearly love, is in a home now, and I make sure that she always gets a birthday card, my books, and I see her whenever I am in Cincinnati, where she lives. I cannot abandon her simply because Mommy is gone. I still visit with my fifth-grade teacher, Sister Augustine, the person who has known me the longest who is not kin, fifty-two years. I have told her she cannot die. It would be too much. I met her when I was ten and needed someone like her in my life. She laughs about it and says, 'You were just not going to let me go,' and I say, 'Well, lucky you! Now you have somebody to talk to.' And we laugh. But I loved her and I do love her. I love Ms. Delaney, my eighth-grade teacher, who would let me read anything and would talk to me. She lived a good long life. As an adult, I would always go back to see her and address her Christmas cards for her. She passed away five years ago.

"I take my friendships and my responsibilities very seriously, as I feel they are linked together. But I have been given a gift now in that I am no longer responsible for the Giovannis. Now it's time to be me. As for my son and nephew, at this point they have to make their own lives. I have seen too many parents live their lives through their children—that is a terrible idea. It doesn't mean that were something were to happen, I wouldn't be there. In a way, children are like spouses. People are together for twenty-five years, they get a divorce, and they say that the marriage failed. On the contrary, I think that perhaps the twenty-five years was sufficient.

"As for how you look at birth, how we bring people into the world, is that a special situation? My answer is no. I was a graduate student in social work, and I am a great fan of adoption. Take Angelina Jolie. She adopted Maddox. She fell in love with the kid and he with her. One day they may not like each other, which won't mean that it wasn't a successful adoption but the end of a relationship."

Being freed of family responsibility, Nikki looks forward to a trip around the world by boat for what she calls the Zoo Project. She plans to look at the work of Charles Darwin through the eyes of a poet in order to better understand and interpret it.

"I'm taking my laptop so I can keep track of everything. A poet watches—it is part of my temperament to pay attention and look at things. I used to think I could remember it all as I traveled, but I won't make that mistake again. What I'm looking forward to is my first twenty days alone at sea. One of the things a writer needs is boredom. People don't realize that. You have to push yourself to the point where you have nothing, because we fiddle, and if we can find something else to do, we will. Finally you end up with nothing to do but to be, and then your mind goes 'kick!' "

This trip has been delayed by Nikki's own bout with cancer, which left her with one lung. With all her losses to cancer, Nikki was in the midst of making a Christmas card that reads "Back Hurt, Cancer Alert, Get your MRI, CT Scan Now! Merry Christmas, Happy New Year" to remind people to be proactive by getting checked. She noted that 70 percent of all cancers include the experience of back pain.

With thoughts of Darwin still lingering in the air, Nikki mentions that recently a scientist who was a fan of hers had written for permission to name a bat that lives in the

mountainous forest of Chile after her. So now there is a bat officially named MICRONYTERIS GIOVANNIAE. *"He said its big ears and its little eyes that see everything made him think of me,"*
she laughs, "so if nobody remembers my poetry, there will still be the bats."

Our conversation turned to fashion. At the moment Nikki was wearing her hair cropped very short and frosted blond, with one side sprayed bright blue, her homage to women of a certain age who in the past rinsed their grey hair blue. She was sporting a St. John pantsuit with an English striped shirt and a necktie in memory of her father, with sensuous, bright-red handmade Spanish leather shoes, and great antique jewelry. Definitely a very individual fashion statement.

"When I was in high school, I knew that clothes were a trap. My grandparents were taking care of me on a limited income, and I couldn't put that burden on them. So I was a beatnik and wore a black skirt and sweater and tennis shoes held together with pins. When I went to college I got an Afro—for a bunch of reasons, but I also knew it made my hair just one less thing to deal with. The same for bras and deodorant. I have come late to enjoying clothes and having fun with them. I like to put my hands in my pockets, and I just got a great pair of black velvet pants with pockets. I wear them with these bright green shoes."

The neckties hold a story and in a way a healing.

After helping her sister Gary through college, Nikki took her to Paris to celebrate her graduation. While there, they purchased neckties for their father as a present. When he passed away, they both wore the neckties in tribute to him, as in the latter part of his life they had been reconciled after earlier stormy relationships. Nikki came to understand him better and to see him through the eyes of her mother, who had loved him in spite of his drinking and abusive behavior earlier in her life. Once he passed through that period, he brought her happiness. But as a young girl, his behavior had made Nikki fearful and unhappy and was the reason she went to live with her grandparents.

Nikki's son wore the tie for his graduation from Morehouse College. Nikki wore it as a talisman against her nervousness when the Steppenwolf Theatre did a play about her.

Finally she started wearing ties with a shirt and long skirt on campus at Virginia Tech, where she is a professor. And thus evolved a "very English look," as she says.

Some of Nikki's most moving and beautiful poems are about black women, among them poems written in dedication to her mother and to her grandmother, who was a pioneer in the movement for civil rights. She writes for all women searching for love, beauty, and understanding, about their pain and glory, and sometimes about just being silly, dizzy in love, as in one of my favorite Giovanni poems, "I Wrote a Good Omelet." Her poem "A Certain Peace" is one many woman can relate to, about enjoying the peace of time alone and the pleasure and anticipation of a loved one's return. I asked Nikki what she thought made women sensuous and vibrant as we grow in age.

"You know I'm a fan of older black women. I think about the women who were friends of my mother. They wore skirts and aprons, sometimes men's slippers. There was a soulful sensuousness about them, warm and mellow, like bodies swaying, foot-tapping happy blues, that drew you in, and they would say, 'Come here Sugar, what you up to?' It's that 'Come here Sugar' that was so sensual and attractive. I think that genital sexuality is so overblown in America. We are missing the whole thing. Sure, at some point the hormones run, no question about it, but for the most part, when you think about it, it's the touch and the smell that you remember."

As a poet, Nikki knows that she is an eclectic thinker, putting things together that don't always make sense in the real world. "If I didn't write poetry, nobody would understand me," she says. She thinks about going to Mars, and says black people will tell the rest how to survive in an alien land. "Think about it, you came from some village in some African nation broken away from your tribe, your community, your food and rituals. You marched to the coast, got caged in a boat in the most horrible of conditions, never saw anyone or anything that you knew again. And there you are, chopping wood, planting cotton, clearing land in this strange place. How did those people remain sane? It was our incredible spirit, and it is this gift that we brought to America and that prepares us to understand what it would be like to land on Mars!"

Rounding the corner toward Jo Hanson's home, I am buffeted by a fierce wind. This windy street and its blowing bounty of urban trash has been the inspiration for Hanson's work as an environmental artist, activist, and lecturer. I arrive at a stately Victorian that covers three-quarters of the block, wind my way up the path. and ring the bell.

Jo Hanson

Jo Hanson is small, but her presence fills the grand old mansion she rescued from dereliction in the early 1970s all the way up to its high ceilings. The rooms fling wide open, unfurling into each other, a spacious and gracious setting for her art, which is everywhere, some of it totemic in scale, and most constructed from urban trash. From the first moments in the foyer of her home we engage in conversation that nearly keeps us rooted to the spot. Her deep, throaty laugh is infectious. Jo has the ability of an alchemist to turn trash into treasure. Through the eyes of her wit, intellect, and imagination, she transforms castaway objects—most of them recovered from her own street—into things that are memorable and magical. A horse's bit becomes a pair of eyes, a doll's torso is collaged with street detritus into a powerful and terrifying visual mantra.

The entry foyer is dominated by part of an enormous installation that was originally exhibited at the Corcoran Gallery in Washington, D.C. Huge transparencies, photographic enlargements of trees that appear to be in motion, cover the walls, shimmering in the changing light and throwing up haunting, ghostly flickers, images, and patterns. Memorial stones are placed on the floor in front of this panorama. It's one of the few things not inspired by trash, but by a visit to a cemetery that was a part of the Crab Orchid Church in the area of southern Illinois where Jo was born and where she later discovered that many of her relatives were buried.

"WHEN I WAS A CHILD, I WAS TERRIFIED OF DYING. My mother was a quilt-maker, and her group of ladies would sit around the quilt telling folk stories while I played underneath. One of the favorite ones was of people who were saved from death by knocking on their coffins just as they were about to be buried alive. Just the thought of it would suck all the energy from me, and I would pray to God to never let me die. While I was unconscious of it when I created the cemetery piece, this was one of the ways of losing my fear of death.

"We belonged to a sect called Hillerites, which had a very fundamentalist interpretation of the bible. I wasn't interested in any of it, going to church, prayer meetings, Sunday school, and the like. The benches were hard. They weren't talking to me, and I truly disliked it. About the age of twelve I learned about evolution, which seemed more reasonable to me, and I became a very committed atheist. At a certain point I became an agnostic.

"In about 1970, I injured my back, and through a series of events I started doing yoga. It didn't cure my back, but I noticed that I would find myself crying in the middle of class. I learned about tissue stimulation of emotional centers. Having recently divorced after twenty-five years of marriage, I was in pain, anger, and emotional turmoil. I was beginning to understand the mind-body connection and was aware that my anger had created the onset of arthritis. Anger is just possibly the most destructive thing I know. The yoga experience and chiropractic were new to me, but they were providing a benefit. I had been dubious about all these things. Following this experience, I heard about the benefits of Huna, the spiritual practice of the Hawaiian people, and thought I would observe a class in it. I discovered that I had to participate to experience it. I approached it with doubt but quickly became a convert. Step by step, this directed me to becoming what I now call a spiritual person.

"I use the terms spirit and energy alternately. It's something we and everything that's living are connected with. No matter how tangled or diverse, we are part of this web. That was a dramatically different approach to living for me, and it has become increasingly important in my life. I feel we need to understand that everything we do is putting something in the world. This blows my mind, just to say it. If I put the wrong stuff into the web, then I'm making it worse for everybody. You constantly need to make value judgments—Is this what you want to live with or your children to inherit? The Iroquois judged an action this way: How would it affect people seven generations later? I think you have to understand that whatever you do or say, whatever you think, you're making the world with it. Do you want people to love or to hate, fight or negotiate?"

Our conversation turned to art as I observed Jo's vast, sunny studio, just past her book-filled kitchen (she's addicted to reading) and facing her garden. The studio is filled with objects waiting to be transformed with buzz saws, lathes, and other tools. She mentions the pleasure she had as a young girl helping her father with various tasks and how she learned by watching. Every experience contributes to the next thing, and as an artist Jo has harvested her experiences as teacher, social worker, and journalist for her work. "I don't separate my life from my artistic work," she says. "The work draws from and reflects my life."

When Jo's neighborhood fell into urban blight she understood that this created an environment for crime. She started sweeping her street, and then her block, as a way of creating a sense of order and caring out of the chaos. She began collecting some of what she found, and her life as an artist broadened to include ecological issues. Her awareness of the waste in our urban society emerged in collage, sculpture, installations, and events concerning sources and dispositions of trash and its assault upon Mother Earth. She became an arts commissioner for the city of San Francisco and created an arts program with San Francisco's disposal company to promote public awareness and waste reduction.

As we talked, I was reminded of how often we have the opportunity to make a difference if we just focus on what is right in front of us. When Jo lived on the Russian River, she was able to observe the intelligence of nature, and her work expanded to include restoration of native growth and creek bank restoration. This led to an installation called GAIA DOES THE LAUNDRY, influenced by her experience of major flooding. She believes that care for the earth, for people, and a positive role in society are all tied together.

"I decided in my twenties that age had no meaning, so I never celebrated birthdays. In fact, I didn't remember the day unless someone mentioned it. Have you noticed that only in America do we identify people initially by their age? It's such a limiting concept.

"My life as an artist went into full throttle as I reached my sixties. What I was doing, thinking, the work, the outcome, it was a time of flowering and expanding, and I liked it enormously. There was a time when I couldn't draw, and after a series of experiences I found that I could. I was in school again, enrolled in psychology and taking an art class. After a couple of semesters, I stopped pretending about my interest in art and worked at it full time, which impacted my marriage.

"As a young woman I never intended to marry, but as I looked around it seemed that women who were married were having a better time of it. There was a man I really liked, so I proposed, and he accepted! When we divorced it was devastating. I thought that there were not many unmarried men. I was at a reception chatting across the buffet table with this man who was a well-known painter, and as we were assessing each other he said, 'Are you looking for a husband?' And I said, 'No, I'm looking for a mate.' My response shocked the woman who was standing next to me—this was at a time when people were expected to marry. But I began to see that the world was full of unmarried men—who would not make good marriage partners.

"I explored relationships with men my age, men older, some younger, and all were pleasing in one way or another, but ultimately I didn't find a relationship that was as important or rewarding as the work I do. I have wonderful friendships, male and female, but I am not looking for a mate. I would be perfectly happy with a relationship with a woman if it turned out that way. I'm very pleased with what I have. I wouldn't be happy if I were isolated and without a community, but I like autonomy, being able to change my mind. I want to summarize what I have done and that takes a lot of time and energy."

Our conversation about relationships led to talking about family, and I asked Jo about her experience of having children.

"I learned how to be a parent, which I certainly didn't know before! I learned so much about love from my daughter as she was growing up. Not that she was loving all the time, but observing her, her relationships with people, with animals, and so on, I saw love in a way that was new to me. It was an enlightening process. I also began to think about children's autonomy and about how to respect their individuality. It's my observation that when decisions are being made that affect a child in a significant way, they should be a part of the decision-making process. They may not have the final voice, but at least their thoughts are included. I didn't have that experience when I was a child. When my son came along, he benefited from all I had learned."

Toward the end of our time together, our conversation rambled over a number of subjects. We focused on our society's attitudes about age and how the baby boomers have begun to create a different awareness of women's roles in society.

"I think that participation in government and all its parts equally by men and women is what will make it noble and important when we are seventy and over. Our society has been out of balance for several millennia. It has been male-dominated and controlled. This has exaggerated male qualities to a point that they have become liabilities. We settle things with armament rather than negotiation, we tell lies in government instead of trying to design government to serve people. We need the balance of feminine traits of loving and caring, nurturing, wanting to make things better for people. I don't think these qualities are limited to women. We are all a balance of male and female.

"Recently I went to a conference of the International Museum of Women, an assembly of women from all over the world. They ranged broadly in age, with an emphasis on younger women. They were demanding respect, authority, to have their role in the world, equal salaries and so on. It made me feel that changes are happening that will make a difference. There are many such groups—it's in process, and one can support the process and live it."

And speaking of living, I asked Jo how she felt she would leave the world a better place. She gave me a very unique answer.

"I discovered there are ecological cemeteries in the area, meaning that one can return one's body back to the earth instead of putting it in a metal thing and breaking the pattern of taking and giving back. It's just not decent to relate to the earth and all it has supplied to life and not give back. And I intend to promote this idea!"

Jean Houston has a mythic presence, a persona larger than life. She is an embodiment of Athena, the goddess of wisdom and knowledge, both of which she has in abundance—along with great wit, terrific acting skills, and a good dose of compassion.

Jean Houston

Jean's father was Jack Houston, a comedy writer for everyone from Henny Youngman, Edgar Bergen, and Charlie McCarthy to Jack Benny and George Burns. So Jean was marinated in laughter, exposed to the world at four years old on the back lots of MGM, and before the age of twelve had attended twenty schools in forty-three states. She had the opportunity to observe and study a broad range of humanity with all its shifting variables, adapting, changing, and often shaping people and events with her will and humor as she was enrolled in one school after another and her family journeyed back and forth across the country for her father's work.

During their travels, her mother exposed her to great literature—Shakespeare, Greek classics, poetry, history—and to Italian opera, so in general she was better schooled than most children. She says that her genetic heritage, a combination of Sicilian, Scottish, and Cherokee, adds to this mix. She became a fusion cook at the age of eight, she recalls, because her father loathed the smell of garlic and she was trying to keep her parents together.

Cooking still is one of Jean's great pleasures and talents, along with being able to talk to any dog. At ten, she began reading Joseph Campbell's THE HERO WITH A THOUSAND FACES. *She says she believes that she was "theologically precocious and philosophically deft" at an early age, having had her first mystical experience when she was eight. As an adult, she met Joseph Campbell, and they became colleagues, giving seminars together on the subject of myths, archetype, symbols, and the psyche. From her childhood beginnings, Jean seemed destined to interface with great leaders in all aspects of life, art, literature, and politics, and with great thinkers on the cutting edge. On class excursions while she attended P.S. 6 in New York she met Albert Einstein and had a conversation with Helen Keller.*

On a late spring morning, we flew to Santa Barbara, California, to meet with Jean Houston and to attend a lecture she was giving later that evening. Jean is an imposing figure nearly six feet tall, with a mane of hair framing her face. Wearing a flowing velvet garment and a golden disc with the symbol of Athena around her neck, she informed, cajoled, and entertained a jam-packed auditorium with her knowledge as a scholar, a leader in the field of human potential, a philosopher, and a visionary thinker, switching from English to Greek, French, and Italian, and back, without a pause.

She is an inveterate traveler, having been to over 100 countries and traveling at times 250,000 miles a year, by jet, camel, boat, or any means necessary to be among indigenous cultures and learn the wisdom of their ways. She has worked as an advisor to UNICEF, the Institute of Cultural Affairs, the United Nations, and on projects with the Dalai Lama, and she carries on the work of one of her mentors and colleagues, the anthropologist and cultural historian Margaret Mead. She says that one of the side benefits of all of her travel is that it keeps her marriage of forty years fresh and interesting.

Earlier in the day we spent some time together as she talked about the amazing encounters and influences of her life. She is soft-spoken as she deftly weaves together ideas about the personal and social realms and the paradigm shift she sees occurring with her fantastical experiences and stories. She has packed more living into this lifetime than most people could do in several. I asked about her ability to influence the fluidity of time, a process she teaches in her Mystery School and Social Artistry programs, as well as how she could so clearly remember childhood conversations and events as portrayed in her book A MYTHIC LIFE.

"WHEN I WAS A YOUNG GIRL my father insisted that I always carry a notebook with me, and if anybody said anything interesting I was to write it down. He was always looking for material for a gag. Margaret Mead did the same thing—she carried a little red notebook, a new one for each month, and in the evening she would take it out and reflect on what she had written. So I wrote down everything.

"When I was about fourteen, my parents were splitting up and I was devastated. I was told that the only way you could get rid of grief was to run. We were living in New York again and while running I ran right into this old man, and he said with a French accent, 'Are you planning to run like that for the rest of your life?'

" I said, 'Yes, sir, it looks that way.'

"We saw each other again the following week as I was walking my dog, and thus began my weekly walks with this gentleman I called Mr. Thayer. It was a tremendous experience—the concepts he exposed me to, his sense of reverence, his ability to see beyond the ordinary in everyday life, the inventiveness in him, his sense of wonder. He had a quite an influence on me and some of it is reflected in my work. He would fall to the ground to look at a caterpillar and deliver a soliloquy: 'What is a caterpillar, moving, changing, transforming, metamorphosing? When are you going to become a *papillon,* Jean?'

"I began to read the books he talked about, Alfred North Whitehead's *Adventures in Ideas,* Plato's *Republic.* Years later when I was at graduate school someone handed me a book called *The Phenomenon of Man,* and as I read, it recalled the talks I had with this gentleman during those walks years ago. Then I saw the cover with a photograph, and I realized that my Mr. Thayer was Teilhard de Chardin, the visionary French Jesuit, philosopher, paleontologist, and biologist who believed in the evolving consciousness of the planet and humanity, and our connection heart to heart.

"In graduate school, I met psychiatrists and physicians who had government-sponsored grants to do LSD research. Many of them were running into myths, archetypes, huge stories, symbols. I was studying those things and knew how to recognize the themes. I was invited to join their team and worked with 300 subjects, studying scientifically the effects of the drug on human personality. This was tremendous—I had access to the collective unconscious of the human mind because of the magnification of the psychodynamic process. I could study the phenomenology of the human psyche in ways that would otherwise have taken me years. This was a pretty amazing experience to have at age twenty-two. Then I traveled around the country speaking to kids about the dangers of drugs because Timothy Leary had been running around talking about how great they were. My husband, Robert Masters, and I created a process for exploring human consciousness without drugs, out of which came a book called *Mind Games.* There are ways of exploring the mind, essentially in a self-induced trance, for example, ways to go inward and work with time so that in five minutes of clock time you could accomplish something that normally would take you an hour.

"During this time I was also teaching at the New School for Social Research, giving lectures on William James's work *The Varieties of Religious Experience*. This had come about at the invitation of Professor Henry Kallen, an executor of some of James's coursework, who felt I could teach this in light of my experience doing research into states of consciousness."

I asked Jean about the challenges in her unusual life and what would have been of value to know as a younger woman.

"I didn't understand the tragedy that is part of life, the nature of suffering and rising from the depths, and the wisdom they can bring. Perhaps soulmaking occurs through the wounding of the psyche—often we gain the complexity, the richness to be able to make a difference from that. Depending upon how we deal with the wound, it can bring wisdom or retreat. It can take the form of denial, cynicism, infantile aggression, cloud your eyes and make you refuse to see. For many women it takes the form of deepening. The process of the wounding is part of the larger story of our lives.

"Certainly I know that in ways now that I didn't at the age of seventeen. I was a premature baby, born at seven months, just this tiny thing, and being born early left me literally unfinished. When you come that early, there are certain kinds of sheathings that just don't develop very well. So it left me hypersensitive, which is kind of hard when you lead a very public life. I realized that this gift—or curse, however you want to see it—if I looked at it differently, gave me my strongest quality, which is radical empathy with people, dogs, animals, ideas, and cultures. It allowed me to learn at a deeper level."

Jean and her father had what they called "The Jack and Jeannie Show." They were always thinking up schemes and jokes, some of which Jean pulled off in school and church, scandalizing or endearing her to onlookers or unsuspecting participants. Her father's way of teaching her to ride a two-wheel bicycle was to take her to the top of an incline with instructions to hang on as long as she could. In teaching her to swim at the age of three, he waded out in the water with young Jean on his shoulders then flung her off with the instructions to dog paddle. His constant advice was "Never be afraid of anything!" Losing her father's companionship when her parents separated was devastating for Jean. She had always felt he was her greatest friend and ally, but in his last years he dealt her a significant blow. Having never quite understood what her career was about, in a letter he admonished her about the direction of her work, which Jean said really caused her to have doubts about her own self value.

Margaret Mead told Jean to "go out into the world and harvest the human potential" and gave her letters of introduction to the indigenous elders of many cultures. I asked Jean what significant changes she feels are taking place and what is important now for women to know.

"I believe we are in the process of the most important change in our history of the past five thousand years—and that is the rise of women to full partnership with men in the whole domain of human affairs. There are also good men coming along, with depth, compassion, and caring, who make for wonderful partners. Women, especially women of a certain age, are making a profound difference all over the world. For example, in Kenya there are women who have formed a shadow feminine government and are working eighteen hours a day, whether to take care of a tribe or to orchestrate something around the development goals for the country. Women have a role that they've never had in human history. It's as if they have been gestating this role in the womb of preparatory time all these many millennium, and now it is ready.

"Perhaps the earth has more than a sufficient human population and needs a feminine sensibility to save it. Perhaps it is the feminine face of God rising, blocked too long by patriarchal societies. Or perhaps she rises because we are in need of this level of nurturing, new orders of growth and development. Roles are shifting radically between men and women, and all the rules are being rewritten in new ways. A partnership society is evolving all over the world, albeit with tremendous backlash. Right now there is this great shaking up.

"I hope women will remember they are the generative possibility for the continuance of life on earth—not by having babies, but by creating social structures, communities, relationships that allow for a richer use of our humanity, in the arts, sciences, how we educate, the way we keep ourselves healthy, the way we birth and die. Women are becoming the social artists who weave these parts together with creative vision and innovation."

In the early 1960s, living in Lakeville, Connecticut, as a wife and the mother of five, Barbara Hubbard read Betty Friedan's book THE FEMININE MYSTIQUE and slowly reawakened to the life quest that had fallen dormant while she raised her children. In 1984 she ran for nomination as the vice presidential candidate on the Democratic ticket. Barbara's father was Louis Marx, the most successful toymaker in the world, who as young man had embraced the Horatio Alger belief in the American Dream. Barbara had a very close relationship with her father. When as a young girl she asked him, "What religion are we?" he said, "You're an American. Do your best." He inculcated in Barbara a belief that anyone with the privilege of living in a free nation had both opportunity and responsibility.

Barbara Marx Hubbard

Author and social visionary, president and executive director of the Foundation for Conscious Evolution, Barbara was doing a series of lectures at Esalen Institute in Big Sur, California, when we drove down from San Francisco to meet her. Mother Nature provided us a repertoire of every kind of weather, but as we arrived on the coast the sun was shining over the splendid vastness of the Pacific Ocean. After settling in at the house nestled in the trees that was built on the grounds of Esalen for Fritz Perls, the father of gestalt psychology, we spent the afternoon in conversation sitting in a round room with soaring ceilings and windows that embraced the glory of the ocean. No ceiling could encompass the mind and intellect of this brilliant woman with a blaze of crystal white hair and a palpable focus of thought and articulation. Years ago, Barbara came to understand that her purpose in life was to be the storyteller of humanity's evolution and to create something that would further our evolutionary potential. This has been the focus of her work for the past thirty-five years, with

particular attention to the changing roles of women. I really resonated to the work she was engaged in and wanted to talk about the journey of discovery that led her to this mission.

"MY FATHER REALLY TOUCHED MY SOUL with the belief that everybody has a purpose. I was fifteen years old when America dropped the atomic bomb, and it had a great effect on me. My question became 'What is the purpose of our power, and how are we going to do our best at if we have more and more power that is destructive?'

"This question really drove me and intensified my need to understand my own larger purpose. I searched everywhere for answers, I asked everyone the same question, inquired through books, magazines, the New Testament, talked to the priest at the Episcopal church near my home, took Sunday school classes, and found no images that gave me the hope of a positive future. During my time at church I was especially upset about the way Eve's quest for the Tree of Knowledge was interpreted, as I related strongly to this image.

"I went to Paris during my junior year abroad from Bryn Mawr. I was sitting alone in a café when a young man joined me. I asked him my usual question, and he surprised me by saying that he was an artist and 'seeking a new image of man commensurate with our power to shape the future.' As we talked I knew this was the man I would marry. I graduated from Bryn Mawr with a degree in political science in 1951, wanting to go to Washington and get a job. My new husband wanted me to move to the country with him so he could be an artist, and, being part of the Betty Friedan generation, I did. As soon as I married I lost my identity. I was a wife and then a mother. When I became pregnant with my first child, I remember so clearly resenting the pregnancy at first. But when the milk started to come in, I wrote in my journal that I was being reprogrammed by my hormones, and I wanted that baby. I shifted form the urge for self-development to the urge for self-reproduction. As I was nursing, all past desires vanished from my conscious—but when the baby was weaned, the desire to find my purpose would come back.

"I began to interpret these feelings as something wrong with me. Why am I not happy? I thought. I should be. I was fulfilling the American Dream. I looked around Lakeville, Connecticut, and couldn't find anyone who was happy—nobody seemed to have a deep purpose. The women were having all these babies, the men were pretending to be farmers, everyone was trying to have a good life. What I learned from all the babies, as much as I loved them, is that for a woman like me who is programmed with a deeper soul purpose, mothering alone will not make you happy. I loved my children a lot, but by the time I had my fourth child I had sunk into such a deep depression I felt that I couldn't speak or relate to anybody. My own voice was echoing in my head, and I was trapped internally. I was cooking, cleaning, taking the children to school, loving my husband and children, and feeling that I was dying. Many years later, my children told me that although I was with them all the time, they never felt I was really there.

"I was born into a set of ideas, a mimetic code of the agnostic, material, competitive culture, which had no reference to this quest for meaning in my own life, and, without guidance, my soul, which needed to express itself, couldn't find an outlet. What finally happened was that I was liberated by a set of ideas. There were several masterful thinkers who freed me, the first being Betty Friedan. All these women she interviewed for her book seemed to be like me. They had lost their identity, had no image of themselves after the age of twenty-one other than wife and mother, and so many of the women, mostly well-educated, were falling into this depression—'the disease with no name,' as she called it.

"Then I read the work of Abraham Maslow, one of the most important figures of the Human Potential Movement, and got the key thought that every person who achieved full potential shared something in common, and that was chosen work that expressed their creativity. So I understood that I had something emerging in me, but there was no affirmation of this feeling, and I had not found my vocation. I loved my children, but, shockingly, motherhood was not my calling. I no longer felt neurotic, just underdeveloped.

"Teilhard de Chardin, a Catholic Jesuit and paleontologist, is one of the great masters of evolutionary consciousness. He believed that as humans continued to evolve, more and more of us were expanding to a divine consciousness, and that the time would come when we would all be connected heart to heart. When I read his book *The Phenomenon of Man,* it struck such a deep chord in me that I was able to identify my own urge for greater consciousness, freedom, and connectivity as the universe in me was evolving. He said that those who felt an emerging towards this unknown had a feeling like a flame of expectation in their hearts, and that if you met one another in a room full of people nothing could keep you apart. I read Sri Aurobindo, Teilhard's eastern counterpart, and Buckminster Fuller. So I was filled with all these thoughts and ideas, but I had never met another such person. They were not in Lakeville, Connecticut, that I knew of, not at the PTA or the League of Women Voters, and I felt so out of it.

"I wrote a letter to Dr. Jonas Salk about a project he was working on at the Salk Institute, and I got a call one day—I'll never forget it. I was sitting in the garden with my fifth child, the phone rang, and he said, 'Mrs. Hubbard? This is Dr. Jonas Salk; we are two peas in the same genetic pod. You have written my heart's desire. Could I take you to lunch?'

"This was 1964, I had just read all these thinkers, and I was just overflowing. When he picked me up, it was a beautiful September day. We looked at each other as I opened the door, and he said, 'This is like the Garden of Eden,' and I said, 'Yes, and I'm Eve, and I'm leaving.'

"This was an encounter of the highest order, and driving to New York I told him everything that was wrong with me, this desire for the future, this need to connect, this sense that something more was coming. He said, 'Barbara, that's not what's wrong with you. It's what's right with you. You combine the characteristics needed by evolution now. You are a psychological mutant, and I will introduce you to a few others.'

"Tears were pouring down my face. I was so happy. Every evolutionary woman, every emergent universal being, needs to find at least one other that can recognize you and be seen. It's much easier now, but it was not easy in the 1960s. There was no environment for it, so when Jonas introduced me to a few others I was doubly ecstatic.

"I feel that a new species, the universal human, is emerging now. The characteristics are that we connected through the heart to the whole of life, we feel awakened from within by this passion to express uniquely for the good of the self and the whole, we are not our tribe, our gender, our color. We are part of the whole continuum, within each one of us is the universe. We have higher guidance and the ability to listen internally. Since I was affirmed, my whole life has been about sharing this, so that others would be able to know that there is a context, a purpose, and a meaning for their lives.

"I've come to believe that women have a great sensitivity to this new time that is emerging, and one of the reasons, I believe, is that our bodies are capable of the miracle of reproducing our species. When we get turned on by a deep vocational call or life purpose, our bodies, our hormones, our entire beings get activated, and we are here now to give birth to this authentic feminine self.

"It's not about personal ambition, a profession, a better job. It's why you are here on earth. And so the creative force that was birth can now give birth to this evolutionary self. The process happens more easily after menopause as the body is no longer producing eggs and that energy is freed up so it can have the same passionate power as motherhood. This is the reason that many women ages fifty, sixty, seventy, are so extraordinary. The change in identity for this evolutionary post-menopausal woman is huge. I have coined a word for this change, regenopause. In my seventies, while my body is declining, my spirit and vitality are rising. The evolutionary potential seems to be growing. I don't feel old, I don't feel young, I feel new.

"The planet is out of equilibrium. At the head of most structuring institutions, nation-states, universities, global corporations, and organized religions is the wrong ideology. You don't get to be the head, particularly the head of a nation-state, unless you are good at domination and control. This is the power of the collective ego that the heads of things have. There have to be members of the planet who wake up and guide this power for the sake of life. It is awakening in millions of us now that something new is needed. To continue with more power will lead to total destruction. It has been my experience that most people waking up to this fact are women over fifty."

Barbara had communicated so clearly what so many of us feel, this experience of passage into something new. Books, conversations, people, pivotal experiences sometimes painful and at times wonderful, all lead the way. A small flame in the darkness ignites in us a more enlightened, evolved, and conscious self. Our conversation returned to the meeting with Jonas Salk, a critical moment in her development. I wanted to know how she integrated this affirmation of her emerging new self into her life.

"I became what I call vocationally aroused, turned on by creativity, and began to move out into the world. I started working with Jonas on a project. I was still in the mindset of the time, woman helping man.

"This new creativity from my reading, meeting Jonas and his friends, reverted to my love for my husband, who was stimulated by my questions and our dialogues, and also influenced by them in his work as an artist. We were able to affirm the reason for our marriage and our five wonderful children and to shift as a couple from procreation to co-creation.

"By the way, most of my deepest creativity has flowed in a profound partnership with a creative man. Whether or not the relationships were exactly right in human terms, they were correct in evolutionary terms. So my marriage was fruitful in every way, and that is to be celebrated. I don't think it means that you have to stay together and inhibit each other's growth. I came to the point where I felt that I had something to say, and the role of being helper for the man just did not work. It wasn't that I didn't love and admire him. He could not make me happy, which was shocking to him. I had to do that for myself. I eventually divorced my husband and took my five children to Washington. I feel that my marriage was successful, but I couldn't fulfill my mission its context."

Barbara continued to describe the myriad cosmic experiences that confirmed for her that she was doing the work she was meant to do. It led to her involvement in and founding of many organizations that would further the development of evolutionary transformation, including the World Future Society, New Dimensions Radio, Women of Vision in Action. In the 1970s she co-founded The Committee for the Future in Washington, D.C., and in 1984 she decided to run as a Democratic candidate for vice president of the United States.

"With the influence of Buckminster Fuller and others, I decided to make a run for the nomination. I don't know how I had the courage to do this now. I said that we needed a new function in the office of the vice president, an office for the positive future, and a peace room that would be as sophisticated as the war room. It would track innovation breakthroughs and solutions.

"So I declared, put a campaign together, and wrote to all my friends and asked if they would give an event for me. I went all over the country, and everywhere I went I offered these ideas: We're being born toward a universal life, we have creative potential, and America should be identifying what's emergent. And these positive future centers formed everywhere. Remember, this was over twenty-five years ago, before the internet.

"When it was time to go to the convention in San Francisco, my friend urged me not to go. I would be lost, no media, no passes to the floor. The media couldn't pick me up because I was positive—I wasn't against anything. We were ignored by the Democratic party because they thought we were narcissistic human potentialists. However, my guidance was to complete my mission, and I needed two hundred delegates. Having majored in political science, I knew how ridiculous this was, but we all prayed, visualized, meditated, and I made it. At 5:30 in the morning, I got thirty seconds to make a speech, and as I was walking up to the podium the guard said to me, 'Now, Honey, they won't pay any attention to you. They never do. You're saying this for the universe.'

"There were two women whose names were placed in nomination in 1984, mine and Geraldine Ferraro's. When you have a vision that seems way beyond the current reality, that's the time to declare it with conviction and move on it while making friends with current reality. After this huge experience, I was divorced, my children were grown up, away or in college, my life partner of twelve years had died, and I was alone. I wasn't a real politician. I couldn't hold the centers together. So I went to a monastery in Santa Barbara and went into meditation to ask what I was to do now. This was really a dark night of the soul. My guidance was to remain silent until my self-centered mind could be absorbed by my God-centered mind.

"My work these last twenty years has been to see if I can do that, to come to a place where I would not be separate from Source. From this I learned many things. I am at peace and no longer feel a sense of failure that I might not complete my mission. I've learned not to be attached to form, not to live in a sense of urgency of time running out. My book *Emergence* chronicles my experience. I have learned in the deepest sense that the ultimate reward is an internal reward, union with the divine, the evolution of the self, and communion with others."

A number of things have given Barbara a sense of accomplishment and joy. Her life partner is a man with whom she can co-create equally. The centers that she has long envisioned are coming together through her Foundation for Conscious Evolution and her Web site, Evolve: A Global Community Center. Her foundation recently released the first DVD in a documentary series called Humanity Ascending, *in which Barbara chronicles the evolutionary journey of our species.*

On a crisp fall Saturday morning in San Francisco, I park and cross the street to Dolores Huerta's foundation offices. This legendary Latina was cofounder, with Cesar Chavez, of the United Farm Workers and has spent most of her life in the world of collective bargaining and organizing, championing the rights of laborers, while at the same time bearing and raising eleven children. The foundation named for her trains organizers to go into minority farming communities, gather people in the intimate setting of homes, and teach them ways of working together to improve their lives. In an arena dominated by men, she is a powerful presence, with fearless intention and flashing eyes. Her accomplishments are testament to what one individual can do with focus and a belief in something bigger than herself.

Dolores is known for boundless energy, and today is no exception. She has just arrived from a flight, and our meeting is one of many she will have well into the evening before she flies off to her next speaking engagement. We settle into a corner in her office and she immediately begins to talk about an issue that is much on her mind, the subject of sexism and its affect on women in the Latino community.

Dolores Huerta

" SEXISM is one of the big challenges women have in general, and when you're a woman of color you get both racism and sexism. Being able to identify sexist behavior, recognize it for what it is, and realize that it's not good is really important. I had such trauma when I went to work for the farm workers because I was unable to identify it. I wish I had understood it as a young woman, as I would have been able do much more. Understanding it made me a lot stronger. For example, one of the vice presidents was holding back a girl's pay because he wanted her to have sex with him. I became very outspoken and brought the issue up in a meeting and he was chastised for his behavior.

"It's the way women are treated. Nobody listens to what they have to say, they're put down verbally or with body language. What they do is not rewarded, but if a guy does the same thing he gets a lot of recognition. At organizing meetings sponsored by the foundation we see women who won't answer a question but turn to their husbands for the answer. Women have to become aware of sexism, learn to identify it, and acknowledge it before they can understand the effect it has on their lives—whether it's the system, their relatives, or a husband who's treating them badly. Just count the ways women in general have been conditioned by society to feel they have to be dependent on or affirmed by men. You see women acting against their own self-interest, particularly in politics and the church, because they look to a male authority like 'daddy.' I made a decision while I was on the executive board and one of the women asked, 'Does the executive board know?' I had to remind her that I was on the board and while I was not a man I could make a final decision. If you haven't been independent, you've got to declare your declaration of independence!

"A large number of farm workers are women, especially in certain crops like grapes, tomatoes, and oranges. When going through the contracts, I made sure that the women got equal pay. I would have to remind the men when it came time to administer the contract to have women on the committee. My role was also trying to bring other women to the executive board. At the time that Cesar passed away we had the board almost equally balanced with only one more man. I would have to get the women to take the position as they would be fearful, not see their own value as decision makers, not feel qualified, or their husbands would have to come to every meeting with them. One of the women got married and her husband made her leave the board and the union. Power, possessiveness, and domination play a big part in this. Watching out for the girl's virginity is a big deal in the Latino community. One of my granddaughter's friends got a full scholarship to UCLA and she was not allowed to go. Girls are told they have to be careful, to be safe, a boy has to take care of you, to the point that women will let men beat them and won't bring charges against them. These issues are among the main topics I speak about.

"Another issue for young women of color is the whole beauty thing, because in our society indigenous beauty is not celebrated. There is still a focus on European beauty. I was watching a commercial about making your face look thinner with makeup. What's wrong with a plump face? Young women get these messages that make them feel even more inferior. They believe all they have to offer is sex, and that creates teenage pregnancy—and then they're further dominated because their self-esteem and sense of worth is so low. Also, in the Latino community, parents don't talk about sex to their kids. The subject is still somewhat taboo.

"It's often people you love, in your own family, who are sexist. My mother was an incredible woman and the dominant person in our family. She made sure my brothers and sisters shared equally in household chores. She owned a restaurant, ran a hotel, and was a community activist. I was shy as little girl, and she was always encouraging me do things, Girl Scouts, church groups, dancing lessons. When I was about twelve, my mother remarried. Here was a woman capable of running her own life and business who was dominated by her husband until she became so disempowered that she was barely able to make a phone call. When she finally got a divorce, he took half her business. She had been so crushed that she had to reclaim herself from that experience.

"As for ageism in our society—recently I was at a conference in Atlanta about starting a movement to fight against the incarceration of our youth. Harry Belafonte opened the conference. Some Native Americans had said to him, 'Before you do anything, talk to the elders.' So he had called us all together to talk—Julian Bond, Andy Young, Congresswoman Barbara Lee, Charles Rangel, Marion Wright Edelman, Cornell West. It was an incredible meeting, and the next one will be with the young people. If we could promote that idea of talking to the elders first, it would be wonderful. Unfortunately, in our society we have a disrespect for older people, especially older women."

I ask Dolores what happens to older women farm workers, and she says they work so hard that they age quickly.

"It is very painful for Latino families to put a relative in a convalescent home. Often the older women take on the grandchildren—and there's a big difference between being a grandmother who is the caretaker in the home and a grandmother who has been out in the world! I'm not able to be with my grandkids because I'm too busy running around doing activist work. When they do stay with me, they cook and clean just like my own kids did.

"Women have to step up, not just take care of their brothers, fathers, and extended family. We've been taught to keep our place. I say to women, 'No, you have to get in there, be a butinski. When you see something is not right, even if you get criticized, don't wait to be invited, our voices are needed.' Through the organization

The Feminist Majority and the Feminization of Power Campaign in California, we got women together in little communities and told them, 'You have to find someone to run for office. If you don't, one of you has to.' So we got a hundred women to run for city council, supervisor, state legislator, United States congresswoman, and a whole bunch of them were elected! Some of the male Democrats were so annoyed. 'What are you doing, getting all these women to run for office?' I said, 'Nobody ever says this to men running for office.' You have to fight for gender balance.

"When I speak at the schools, it's the young women who embrace me, who hug me and have tears in their eyes. I gave a speech in Fullerton and a girl came up to me and said, 'When you were here the last time, I came with a friend to hear you speak. I was a gang member, and I'm not a gang member anymore.' After a training session a young man from Mexico enrolled five hundred people in his union. Being able to see people engage, transform, and accomplish something they are going after, this gives me pure joy.

"With the older women, I make it a point when I speak to say, 'I'm celebrating my fifty years of organizing and my seventy-five years of birth.' It's wonderful, because women will come up to me and say, 'Well, I'm seventy-three,' or 'I'm eighty.' All of a sudden women start acknowledging their age. We all wish we looked like we did in our twenties, but I think we have to accept ourselves as we are now and learn to love our wrinkles or that extra weight.

"A few of years ago, I had an aneurism and was sick for a year. One appreciates life after a big illness. You know that you have to take the time to do the things you want to do. Not that I have done that but I'm planning to! During this time I thought it was a good moment to let my hair go grey. On my mother's side everybody went grey in their twenties and thirties. Other aunts had jet black hair and they were twenty-five years older than me. My children range in age from their twenties to their early fifties. My young kids thought it was a great idea to go grey, but the ones in their forties didn't. But I think I need to do this if I say I'm going to honor the signs of age, right?"

We both laugh at this crossroad so many of us reach. Then I ask Dolores how she handled her large family and her work at the same time.

"I'm a child of the forties and fifties, and I was raised the old-fashioned way— you had to be a virgin and all that stuff. I had my last four children between the ages of forty and forty-six. I had them in batches, as I have been married and divorced twice. My first marriage was at age nineteen. I think my forties and fifties were probably the best years of my life. I really grew into my womanhood and sexuality, and I was having kids! Women have a responsibility to take part in civil life. It gets us away from being dependent on men when we see another world. You can't get tied to home and hearth because home will never end.

"My mother once said to me that you make a decision on the basis of what will make a difference fifty years from now, and that's how I make decisions. Home was never the focus of my energy. I learned so much, on all levels, from politics and organizing. You have to learn about people to deal with them, and my experience has taught me a lot. My kids were pretty resourceful and involved with what I was doing. If anything, I regret that I wasn't able to do more for them. When we started the United Farm Workers Union there was no money, so I couldn't provide my children with the things I had, like music and dancing lessons, and I feel sad that they never had those opportunities.

"A great thing about growing older is how much more you know from all your life experiences. I've been around a long time. I knew a lot of these politicians before they became great. You develop personal relationships, perhaps you may have had a good fight here and there. There is nothing wrong with conflict over issues. Sometimes you can't resolve things without it, and from it you often become really good friends. As women we must learn to stand together and not play the power games men play on each other to get ahead.

"For women, I think it is important that they be fulfilled—that's true for me anyway. You have to have a purpose in life. When you're a very young woman, relationships with men are very important. But now for me, it's what I leave behind. It's passing on the knowledge I have gotten so that my kids and other people are assisted and are in a good place when I'm gone. I'm still married, and the time I take for my husband and kids gives me the support to go out and do what I do. I love to dance, we have great parties, all my family loves music and dancing. My brother has eleven boys. I have fourteen grandchildren and five great-grandchildren. The whole family gets together and it's wonderful! I was dancing last night."

Dolores exudes the ageless quality that comes from being fully engaged with life. As she says, she will stay involved as long as the good Lord gives her the energy and health to do it. And I'm sure she'll be dancing through it all.

Never one to sit on the sidelines thinking "one day, some day," Beverly Baker Kelly has lived life to the fullest, inhaled experience like a heady perfume. Wife, mother, career woman, and adventurer, she found a way to do it all, smacked the way it should be into the cosmos, and grabbed her star of life.

Beverly Baker Kelly

"FOR SOME WOMEN it's spas, manicures, and massages. This doesn't turn me on, but, Honey, take me to Ethiopia or Timbuktu with the sand up to your tits and I'm in seventh heaven. I like the adventure, I love being fearless, finding a place to stay, learning a language, getting from one place to another, staying well. Trying to see and understand as much of a culture as possible and where a society is on the continuum of the world, it just lights me up.

"When I'm sitting in an airport being a voyeur into the world of others, looking at women wrapped in all that cloth wondering what their lives are like, I'm feeding myself. A man in purple robes comes and says, 'Meez Kelly, I am your driver. Come with me.' And I know that I am off to something interesting. My dreams dry up if I'm away from this too long. India, Sri Lanka, Pakistan and Bangladesh stand out in my mind as real adventures. Recently I was in Liberia for the run-off election as an international election monitor for the Carter Center and the National Democratic Institute. This was a historic moment, as Ellen Johnson-Sirleaf became the first woman to ever be elected president of an African country. I had the opportunity to spend time in conversation with her and a number of officials in this new government. She was especially insightful as she shared her vision for the future of the country she has been elected to lead."

I caught up with Beverly at her home in the East Bay of California, on one of the rare occasions that she was not rushing to catch a plane somewhere. Her dining table was covered with massive briefs—she has a private legal practice in public international law and international child abduction under the Hague Convention and the Center for Missing and Exploited Children. With four master's degrees, two doctorates, a law degree, and a far-flung practice, she found a way to combine her lust for adventure and education very early in life. Between her work and that of her husband of over forty years, who travels for his work in academic medicine, she has spent much of her life spinning around the world.

Beverly grew up the only child in a middle-class African American family in Detroit, feeling somehow that it was incumbent upon her to continue the family legacy of pursuing the American Dream, and that she had to do well. Her parents were teachers and administrators. Her grandfather and uncle were both lawyers, and she was inspired to become one as well.

"I grew up with a group of close girlfriends, and we all went off to college and then got married. As a young woman I always felt like I was a little odd, that I didn't quite fit in. When I went away to college I became, and still am, a loner of sorts. Being an only child shaped my life, as I learned to love others but not need them too much. I learned to feed my mind and be my own best company. I seemed to have a different take on life. I wanted to continue my education, expand my world and my horizons while being married and having my children travel with me wherever my heart desired. My attitude was that my children came to live with me, and it would be better for me to fulfill my goals than to stop life and try to live a more traditional role. I didn't want to wait until I was too old to drag my suitcases around the world.

"I was lucky to marry this wonderful man who understood my inner yearnings and gave me the room to expand. We had two dates and got engaged and I was married six months later at the age of twenty-three. I had never lived on my own, never had an apartment, had not lived life except as a student. While raising my daughters, I had the opportunity to work for UNESCO in Paris for one year—I got paid one dollar per month. So off I went with the girls. We had a nice new empty apartment and I made the furniture from cardboard boxes, white adhesive, and loads of draped material. We sold our car to pay the rent. We lived in Vienna while I was at the John Hopkins International School of Affairs, one year in Italy, and later in London while one of my daughters was at the London School of Economics. Mind you, my husband was not interested in this lifestyle, but he came frequently for visits."

I asked Beverly what she had learned from her children, especially parenting them as she did.

"There was a time when they longed for an Ozzie and Harriet family. They brought me to my knees and made me feel I wasn't parenting right. It was a real push-pull internally. I wanted to take care of their needs, but I wanted slices of my life for myself. I needed to compete in the world of business during the day and also pack lunch boxes, write notes to the school, plan way ahead for summer camps and next year at school, order clothes, plan for all the holidays and birthdays, and keep my husband's schedule in order. I wanted them and I wanted me.

"You need to have your own passion. I needed to take two summers off to write my dissertations, so I learned to juggle and find help. I learned that you never lose your daughters. Though for a period of time, while mine were spreading their wings and telling me to get the hell out of their lives so they could make their own decisions, I felt that we would never see eye to eye again. They now understand that I was just different from most moms. They like, love, and admire this mom and realize how rich their lives have been.

"Material possessions have never been important to me—new cars, making pots of money—and my husband felt the same way, so we found ways to have what was meaningful and important to both our lives. They say you should follow your dreams and the money will follow—but so far I've not found a pot of gold! We are both passionate about what we do. His research base is in southern California, so having a dual career commuting marriage became a way for us to achieve our goals. It's kept our marriage satisfying, fresh, and vibrant. Over the years we have grown in compassion, and when we get to travel together we have a ball.

"The civil rights movement and affirmative action proved to be a real catalyst and changed the direction of my life. I could never have gotten into Harvard's doctoral program or Boalt Hall School of Law without affirmative action. I have been true to my calling ever since, working *pro bono* to help those who are unable to solve their legal problems. My world travel creates a broad perspective and gives me a clearer view, whether I'm working on a child abduction case or am part of a legal tribunal. I love winning cases for my clients.

"My biggest challenge is time management. I have a spacey mind and need long periods of concentration, alone. My temperament is such that I don't work well in other people's systems. I am not a team player, and office politics just wear me out. I just like to work, work, work, without all that drama. I hate to have clashes with others unless I am running interference for one of my clients. I love figuring out a system and how to win in different worlds. Over time I have learned to believe in myself, to trust my instincts, and I'm never afraid that my senses will fail me.

"When I am away and see women walking for miles carrying a little bit of water, it reminds me to turn off the faucet when I'm brushing my teeth at home. Here our roads are paved, not covered in dust. We press a button, and our lights come on, and we think we are entitled to this abundance. It is so easy to get comfortable with America's wealth and I fear that I will forget how others live with so much less every day."

Beverly is the kind of friend who calls you in the wee hours of the morning from some remote place in the world just to stay in touch or to tell you an interesting story, sends Valentine cards in January because that's when she has a moment to do it, or sends an e-mail telling you about the latest thing she has heard about to improve your health. We have had many a conversation about remaining intellectually challenged and not being influenced by negative media images as we grow in age.

"I'm not sure I knew that I had turned sixty—I think too much is made of birthdays. So what if you are a year older? And while I won't hide my age, I'm just not thinking about it. My motto is to not find negative things to say about myself, because in ten years I will probably look back and say how marvelous I was looking way back then.

"Now I know my stock is going down on the 'pretty-stock exchange' and my legs don't look like they did when I was twenty. But that's okay. I'll enjoy the people who think of me as a sophisticated woman of value.

"My parents and their friends started to think about retirement at this age, but I'm just beginning. I plan to work till I'm a hundred, and to live life to the fullest. I used to think that as people grew older they resigned themselves to a life of calm with no agenda. None of these preconceived ideas is true. Of course, health is always a factor, but I'll keep my fingers crossed. I have lived life by the Braille system, feeling my way through. I just want to keep the brain cells working.

"What skills do we as women need for the next forty years of life? I know I won't be buzzing around the kitchen making meals. Keeping up with technology is a challenge for me. I mean what is a terabyte? Getting a handle on where we are historically inspires me. Freidman's book *The World is Flat* is an eye opener, and I'm trying to understand how these concepts will be lived out over the next quarter century.

"Society has no other recourse but to deal with people sixty and older. To change attitudes and perceptions when someone makes a disparaging remark, call them on it. Reinventing retirement, rethinking usefulness, and building skills must be goals for people sixty and over so that society can use these years creatively and constructively. Awareness is essential. We need to know more about the contributions people sixty and over make to this world."

Winding up a steep road on a sparkling spring morning I arrive at Elaine Kim's home high in the Oakland Hills of California, where in 1991 many homes, including Elaine's, burned to the ground in a fire that raged out of control. The area is completely rebuilt, and today Elaine lives in an Asian-inspired home that was designed by one of her former students. The house is decorated with Asian antiques and ethnic art from her world travels and has cozy areas to curl up in with a good book. Sunshine streams in from windows with picture-postcard views of San Francisco and the bay spreading out below.

Elaine Kim

The first thing I do is remove my shoes at the door and don a pair of slippers from the basket that is just inside. American-born of Korean heritage, Elaine is brilliant, passionate, and conversant in her convictions from years of study and research. Her beauty and lithe movement belie the media image of a woman in her sixties. Born in the year of the horse, she says that her temperament is fiery, with a dose of impatience that has been a challenge to overcome.

Elaine is an associate dean and professor of Asian American Studies at the University of California at Berkeley, a writer and producer, and the founder of a number of organizations whose mission is to empower the Asian American community.

At the moment she is in her kitchen whipping up delicious cappuccinos, and we talk as she works. I ask her about moments that have been significant in her life.

"THERE WAS AN INTENSE PERIOD between the ages twenty-four and thirty-one that were the building blocks for the rest of my life. The experiences that were really difficult turned out to be the best, really important for my understanding of the world, becoming a better person, more mature and able to cope.

"I was born and grew up on the east coast of Maryland, where we lived in a white working-class neighborhood in the 1940s and 50s. There were very few Koreans in the area, and the images of Asians, especially men, were not very positive. There were lots of Fu-Manchu and Charlie Chan images, and the image of mostly single old men who had never been able to marry because immigration from Korea had been cut off. There had been no women to marry, so there were few young men.

"My dad seemed small and spoke with a thick accent. He was treated with great disdain, and white people pretended not to understand him even though he was very well educated. I thought he was inferior in some way.

"When I was twenty, I went to Japan and Korea with him and realized that he was very fluent in the languages there, was the same height as most men, had the same gestures as everyone else, and was greatly respected. While I was in Korea I began to understand that I had been the object of a lot of racist conditioning. I saw Asian men who were very masculine, handsome, walked and talked with confidence, and that there were a million people who were very self-confident about themselves racially, as they had not grown up in a society where they were the only persons of color in a room full of white people.

"Several years later, when I had just finished my masters degree at Columbia, I decided that I would go to South Korea to learn the language. This was in 1966. I knew little about the country and what was going on there. I discovered that it was extremely poor and was also sending soldiers to fight in Vietnam as they would then get the same benefits for their families as American soldiers. My dad got me a job teaching English in one of the best universities. No one in the department wanted me there—the president had made them take me.

"I didn't really know any Asian Americans and had never fraternized with any young Korean men. By Korean standards, everything about me was wrong. I was too old to be considered for marriage, too big even though I wore a size four or six in American clothing, smoked cigarettes, talked too loud and too much, my feet were too large, I was assertive, gestured, had straight hair when everyone else was permed, didn't speak the language well—half the time I didn't understand what was being said—so I was treated like I was a little stupid. They would look at me and say, 'Oh, over the hill!' I had thought that all men of color would think I was attractive, and now I felt very ugly and unsure of myself.

"All the people I knew in the U.S. who were my age were against the Vietnam War. Then Lyndon Johnson came to visit Korea, and everybody went out into the street and waved American flags—people were carrying on like he was a king—and that was a big shock to me. I did not know the extent to which anti-communist, pro-American education had been woven into everyday life in South Korea.

"With the split between North and South Korea, there was a lot of suspicion, and everywhere there were signs about catching communists and spies. Because I looked weird to them, people thought I was a spy from North Korea. My briefcase was always being examined, and if I went to the countryside the police there would question me.

"I was staying with a cousin who was, like everyone else, living in poverty, and that hardship was an important lesson for me. My parents were not well off in the U.S., but it was not like Korea. I didn't want my cousin to know that I had more than two dresses, as she only had two, one that she hung on a nail and one that she wore. So I wore the same clothes for a week at a time. I could only take a shower and wash my hair once a week, not every day as I was accustomed to doing. I felt so bad for her and realized that except for good fortune it could have been me. It was winter and it was freezing cold all the time, because they don't heat the indoors of classrooms or other buildings. Life was hard for everyone. I had to take the bus and go to work every day. It was especially difficult because of the language.

"AS A YOUNG GIRL, I was treated as if I didn't exist. It was a very bad time for me. My mother acted as though females were inferior to males and didn't count. But by the age of seventeen I had become very attractive and from that time into my early twenties I received much undeserved attention. So there I was, thinking that I was

God's gift to the Western World because I was treated so well in Europe and the U.S. It had seemed that all I had to do was smile and some guy would make what I wanted possible. At the time I believed men had all the power.

"So, I had a real comeuppance in terms of my self-image. There were all these things for me to see, to understand, and think about myself, as an American, as a Korean American, and as a woman. After the year was over, I traveled around the world, and that was even more eye-opening for me. I learned about cultural relativism, which I hadn't understood. I'm still a little anchored in the idea that America is the center of the world, because that is the way it is presented to us, and this country is culturally so influential and powerful.

"Everyone had harped on me all year about being twenty-four and turning into an old vegetable. Korea is a very progeny-oriented society. So when I came back to the United States, I got married to a man I had been seeing. He was white, with a very good family background. My parents realized that I was not a suitable match for a Korean and they felt it was a better match than none at all.

"When I was a younger woman I was convinced there were two things that a woman needed to know. One, you are nothing without a man, and, two, you can't be too intelligent because that would be dangerous for you. I wish I had known then that I don't have to have a man to be okay, and that I don't have to conceal my intelligence. I still have issues with these thoughts.

"So the difficult times have been extremely helpful to me and have given me lessons to live by and things that I can think and write about. Challenges and hardships, divorce, love lost, my parents dying, and of course the loss of my house and all my possessions in a matter of hours in the fire. Horrible as that was, I realized that my things meant less to me than I had thought, and that was great to know. Still, to have this happen when I was over fifty meant that I lost a lot more of my experiences than as if my house had burned down when I was in my twenties."

During the years of building a successful career, Elaine has faced many challenges. In 1981, as a professor at Berkeley, she was the only woman of color to get tenure in a faculty that was 98 percent white and male.

"I was in the Department for Ethnic Studies. It was very challenging to be in that environment and be a single mother as well. I wasn't sure what was expected of me, as I had no role models, so I threw myself into my work. I was always comparing myself to the men. Of course they were all married and had wives at home, and that allowed them more time to focus on their careers. I also threw myself into community work."

This brings us to the question of family and children, and I ask Elaine about her own experience of mothering.

"I probably should have given my son more of my attention. One thing I learned from raising him is that he's a separate individual from me, with his own wants, desires, and tastes. I have learned to respect those differences, which was quite a step for me, as I had very definite ideas of what he should be and do. It was a good lesson to learn. When he was in high school he used to say, 'Oh, wouldn't it be great to be a dad?' I didn't understand what he meant and thought he didn't get the responsibility of having a family. He is married now, has a successful career, and loves being a husband and father. They have just had a second baby. Our values are not that different, they just manifest in a different way. I was more focused on having a career.

"I continue to learn and grow from my relationships. I learned a great deal from grappling with my relationship with my daughter-in-law, becoming more tolerant and conscious of her point of view, what she wants. It brought me a lot of happiness, a better relationship, and now I am trying to tie those lessons to the relationship with the man in my life. This is so much more vexing, because of my fear of being controlled by men. In past experiences, in my family, my marriage, and the workplace, they exert more power and get much more than women do. And women do all kinds of things to try and make it equitable. So I am working on those feelings."

Elaine talks about the present, what is important to her now, and what brings her the greatest joy in life.

"At this time in my life, emotional intimacy is even more important to me. My granddaughters, my animals, little kids, my son, who is very funny, give me a lot of joy. Being in nature and making love keep me in the present moment and then I am happy and at peace. I don't think much about my age—honestly I feel more attractive now than I have ever felt in my life. I wouldn't want to be other than who I am right now. I have always been one to embrace what gives me pleasure and joy.

"My grad students are also important to me, and I'm very attached to them. They want to see me thrive, as they look to me as a role model, to what is possible for them as women in the future. Many are younger, single, in their thirties, forties, and fifties. They are looking for a sense of what may be possible for them as they grow older, both in relationships and in starting new things. That there is love and intimacy in my life make makes them see that this is possible for them at any age. So I would say, by living and being an example of a possible future, I am creating changes."

As Elaine spoke so candidly about herself, it confirmed my feeling that we needn't be hesitant in expressing our true nature and desires as we age.

As we grow in wisdom, self-confidence, self-love and self-acceptance, being comfortable with ourselves is the result. If we wish to express our vibrant sensuous nature and the full ripeness of our being at this stage of life, we should not hold back.

We become role models for younger as well as older women who fear that growing in age is the end of intimate possibility and pleasure. We are not the women of our mother's or grandmother's generation. The opportunity to explore our feminine qualities can continue to be part of our expression of life at any age. As we were winding down our conversation I asked Elaine about her plans for the future.

"I've been at the university since 1973 and am at the place of thinking about the next step, the next stage for me. But I don't have a clear focus as yet.

"My students give me new ideas, and I enjoy collaboration, like the last book I did. It features twenty-four artists working in a cross-racial, cross-cultural dialogue with different critics, a Filipino artist writing about a Mexican artist, African Americans on Asian artists. As you know, we have all been affected by imperialism and this dialogue is to find out more about each other and the things we share in common.

"The goal of my work has been to try to bring light to some of the things that have been repressed, whether it is art or injustices that happen to people that little attention is given to. These stories are behind the scenes in African American, Native American, and Asian American history. Things that were repressed like the Korean War, where ten million families were separated by the division between south and north, and North Korea was bombed until nothing was left.

"This is part of American history too. If we don't pay attention, these things will come back to bite us. If in some way I have been able to shed light on some facts of history, present a writer, an artist, I hope that this can help to make for more understanding and for the world to be a better place."

"IT WAS ABOUT 8:30 IN THE MORNING, and I was in a meeting at the Capitol—very few members of Congress are around that early—when we received word that a plane was headed towards the capitol and we had to evacuate. People were screaming to get out, get out, now, to run. Run where? I thought. Then I was just running and I saw the smoke coming from the Pentagon. It was terrifying. As it turned out, my chief of staff's cousin was one of the flight attendants on flight number 93. She and the pilot who diverted the plane were African American and from my constituency in Oakland, California. So, for the next days, as this resolution to go to war was being prepared, I was as angry, upset, depressed, and scared as anybody."

Congresswoman Barbara Lee

I am in a boardroom at the Ronald V. Dellums Federal Building in Oakland, California, meeting with Congresswoman Barbara Lee, who arrived to the minute of her appointment with a warm smile of greeting on her face. Her energy is completely focused.

She is co-chair of the Congressional Progressive Caucus, Senior Democratic Whip, and Whip for the Congressional Black Caucus, and serves on the House Financial Services Committee. In 2005, she was nominated for the 1000 Women Nobel Peace Prize. The first thing I ask is how she found the courage to be the only person in Congress to stand up and cast her vote against the war during that terrible time when much of the country was gripped in fear and whipped into the belief that dissent was unpatriotic.

"It was horrible, but knowing what was right and what was wrong, saying my prayers and asking God to give me the strength to weather the storm. At the end of the day I couldn't vote for something that was going to create more violence in the world, nor would I vote for something that I knew was unconstitutional and that would give this or any administration a blank check to wage war. I read the bible, the passage that says, in essence, when the winds are blowing and evil is all around you, just stand and know God will take care of everything.

"There has not been one second when I thought that maybe this was not the right vote. I had to read the resolution, then reread the appropriate provisions in the Constitution, so it was a grueling twenty-four hour process. Then I went to the Master Cathedral for the memorial service, and—I will never forget this—when Reverend Nathan Baxter prayed, 'Let us not become the evil we deplore,' a peace came over me.

"My two sisters and I were sent to a Catholic school, St. Joseph, in El Paso, Texas, and the nuns there were very involved in social justice. Our parents refused to let us go to a segregated school although the all-black school was very good. We ended up being the only black students in the school. It was like living in two worlds, as our neighborhood was only black and Latino kids, but it definitely gave me an insight into white America. My family was very strict. I couldn't talk to boys, couldn't date until age sixteen. All I could do was practice piano, study, read, and go to church.

"I wanted to become Catholic and after much begging and pleading was finally allowed to be baptized into the Catholic Church. Over the years I've grown to understand the power of prayer and of God's intervention in our lives, and that has given me a lot of strength. However, when it comes to politics, I am very clear in my belief in the separation of church and state."

Recently, the Sisters of Loretta honored Barbara Lee for reflecting the values of the Loretta Community, whose motto is "Work for peace, act for justice." They had no idea that she had gone to St. Joseph until they came to meet with her at her office.

"I grew up in a military family. My dad served in Korea and Vietnam, so I know what being a patriot is and the toll it takes on families, what veterans need, and that you only go to war when there is an eminent attack or an immediate need. I think there is still fear in the collective psyche of the American people of another 9-11. This administration has connected a lot of things together that are not really connected, and that has increased that fear. If you look back at history, you'll see that a government can get away with doing anything it wants if the people are fearful enough."

While attending Mills College on scholarship (as a single mother on welfare who often attended classes with her two children at her side), Barbara Lee intended to open a mental health center for the underserved black population in southwest Berkeley. At Mills, she was the president of the Black Student Union. She was convinced that the political system was irrelevant and that she could better bring about reform as a revolutionary working on community projects with the Black Panther Party. She was taking a course in government and was required to work on one of the presidential campaigns but felt that she could not work on behalf of either candidate. She also had never registered to vote. All that changed when the Black Student Union invited Congresswoman Shirley Chisholm from New York City to speak.

"She was the first black woman in Congress. When she came to Mills, she spoke about all kinds of issues, and I listened to everything she had to say. She was just amazing. And then she announced that she was running for president! I went up to speak to her, and the first thing she said was, 'My dear, if you really want to shake things up and really believe in what you say, then the first thing you have to do is register to vote!' I found out she didn't have an organized campaign in northern California, so I got together with Sandy Gaines, who was the Student Union president, and together we ended up organizing Shirley Chisholm's regional campaign out of my government class at Mills, and I got an A in a class I thought I was going to flunk.

"Between my first and second years of graduate school at UC Berkeley I was a capitol intern. I was really struggling to make ends meet. I sent my kids to live with their grandmother in Texas and went to Washington, D.C., to work for Ron Dellums. That was the year of Watergate—it was quite a summer. He invited me to come back and manage his office. I had planned to open my mental health center and had already raised all this money. But after talking about it with a number of friends I realized the opportunity in front of me, and we hired someone else to run the center.

"When I went back to work for Ron, I used to watch Shirley Chisholm. We stayed friends forever—I really loved her, and she would encourage me and show me how to do things. She was the first African American on the Rules Committee and was very powerful. She really navigated that whole house. She said, 'You've got to shake things up. These rules are not made for us. You have got to change the rules. Don't go along to get along.' "

Barbara Lee became Ron Dellums's chief of staff and from 1990 to 1998 served in the California State Assembly and the California State Senate. I asked her what women bring to government that is different from men's contribution.

"I think that women can bring more sanity, sensitivity, intellect, and heart to things because we come with the history of oppression, sexism, and, for women of color, racism. We have a standard for what's good and bad, and you need that in lawmaking.

"In general, men don't have the experience we have. They don't see that cutting childcare is going to hurt a woman who is trying to get through school and that if you cut childcare she could end up on the streets. They may know it intellectually, but when it comes to doing something instinctively, they won't. They will say, 'So what if this woman is forced out, that's life. Let her fend for herself. She should be able to take care of her own kids.'

"Not all men think this way, but most of the ones that run the House and Congress do. As chair of the CBC Task Force on Global HIV/AIDS I have visited areas where commercial sex workers are doing the only thing they can to take care of their kids. These women are desperate for training and jobs. Men will cut money to the very organizations that provide health care to commercial sex workers and try to help them leave the profession on the premise that if they support these organizations they are supporting prostitution. They won't allow them to distribute condoms because 'we have an abstinence-only policy.'

"A lot of sexism and racism is subconscious. When men in power have a choice to make about who benefits, the choice becomes about who's valuable and who's not. It's key that women become more politically involved, both in and out of office—and especially women who don't act like men. But the system sucks you up when you get in, so you have to consciously, every day, remember that the people elected you because you are a woman and have a different point of view. They did not elect me because I am a white guy who will maintain the status quo.

"As women, we tend to fear that we won't fit in and be part of the group, and we have to fight that. We have seventy women in Congress now, and the Women's Caucus includes Republican and Democratic women. There's a supportive environment. Women and children's issues are something we all agree on."

Barbara Lee says that the biggest challenge of her temperament is that she is both shy and an introvert. She is also an artist and as a young woman won musical scholarships for her organ and piano playing. I suggest to her that her creativity may give her an enhanced ability to see and interpret things that are not seen by everyone.

"My mother says that this career is the best thing that could have happened to me. Otherwise I would be off on some island writing poetry by myself. Falling into politics was totally counter-intuitive for my personality. Music, design, architecture—I must have two thousand books on design, every time I have ten minutes I'm drawing something—I love all of it. These things give me a bit of respite and peace. If you are in public life, 95 percent of what you do is public. I think it's very abnormal to always be exposed, it is counter to what the human spirit needs to survive. I wish more public officials would understand that and could chill out and regroup. I think it would make for less mean-spiritedness.

"I have much more patience than I had as a younger woman and it's a good thing because my challenge intellectually is trying to stop all these wars. I'm the most senior Democratic woman on the International Relations Committee, and Condoleezza Rice is the most senior Republican woman, so it's a real challenge in terms of foreign policy. But when you follow what your gut and your heart tells you, you never make a mistake, never!

"I have four grandchildren, twenty-one months to thirteen years old, and it's great. It gives me the affirmation that I'm doing what I should be doing. They call me Bee Bee, which is 'grandmother' in Swahili. They are so interested in what is happening. 'Bee Bee, I saw this yesterday! What'd you do? Did you get arrested in Sudan?'

"This age thing is still a bit of a problem for me. I'm having a birthday in July, the twenty-first anniversary of my thirty-ninth birthday, so don't even ask me about the age thing because that's how I'm dealing with it. Life moves so fast I can't figure it out.

"I think what is important is the path we're on, but you can't be so programmed and organized that you miss out on the diversions in the road. I never planned a career in Congress. You have to be open to the possibilities and trust your inner listening.

"We can make a difference. Every now and then I get a bill passed, and 90 percent of the work of my great staff in Oakland is casework, helping people, whether it's immigration, social security, IRS, housing, you name it. Whether I'm in Sudan or walking down the street in Oakland someone will stop me and say thanks. It makes it all worthwhile."

In 2006, Mills College established the Barbara Lee Distinguished Chair in Women's Leadership in recognition of Barbara's courageous leadership in politics, policymaking, and human rights. In 2007 she was named to the House Appropriations Committee, one of the most powerful committees in Congress.

Sally Lovett's life changed in an instant. While driving to Aspen with her husband she rounded a curve in the road into sudden blinding sleet and a ribbon storm. The SUV skidded onto black ice, rolled, and cartwheeled down the mountain, instantly killing her husband of thirty-six years and crushing both of Sally's legs. She was told she would never walk again.

Today, Sally strides confidently across the living room of her house in Belvedere, California, a place she purchased after the tragedy, one with no memories where she could put back together the shattered pieces of her life. She announces that earlier today she sold this house and will be moving further north to a place where she feels she can again create a feeling of home. Sally is dressed in her characteristically eclectic style, with ethnic jewelry, an embroidered Indian silk shirt, and a classic cashmere sweater tossed over her shoulders. She says she is entertained and amused by the activity of dress. Her maquillage is intentionally riveting. Her strength of intention has made her a powerhouse at directing foundations, developing organizations, and creating her own philanthropic endeavors. We settle into chairs at a dining table that faces out onto the terrace and pool as she begins to recount the events that led to this moment in time.

Sally Lovett

"IT WAS A STRANGE FEW DAYS that led up to the accident. I had been on the Kamchatka Peninsula of the Russian Far East visiting the women's community centers I founded there. Suddenly I became very upset, almost had an anxiety attack, about not being with Bob. This was very unusual for me. But I felt I had to get back so I returned a week early. When I got home I remember how he kept looking at me as if he were really seeing me. He had really missed me. He wanted to leave for Aspen right away. When the accident happened I never lost consciousness, even as my entire life flashed before me. I don't remember being in pain. I kept saying, 'My husband, my husband—' I didn't care about anything else. Usually I didn't even call him my husband. I was helicopter-lifted to a hospital in Reno.

"I miss Bob terribly. He was the most wonderful man, with complete integrity, competence, and total kindness. I wish more than anything that I could have him back, yet I realize that I have become a much more clear, complete, and actualized person having to be alone. Before I could always come running home to Bob. No matter how confident I was in the world, I always needed to check in with him to review that I had made the right decision. He couldn't understand why I needed the reassurance, as I never had any trouble making a decision. I have always been kind of a wild card and a very strong organizer, but somehow I never felt really good about myself.

"With the tragedy and the trauma of reconstructing myself, I had to delve more deeply into parts of my being. I went through all the cycles of grief and depression, including thoughts of suicide. It's pretty common to have these feelings as you are grieving. Life doesn't seem worth living when you are that depressed. At some point during this period I came upon a book written by Kay Redfield Jamison, a professor of Psychiatry at Johns Hopkins School of Medicine. It gave me some understanding of what I was going through and really helped me to shift. I also started using Prozac, which has been wonderful. Nothing else had worked with my chemistry, but for me this was the answer, and I am sure I will use it for the rest of my life. It eliminated that feeling of anxiety and feverishness I always had experienced."

In time Sally joined the community at Spirit Rock Meditation Center in West Marin County, California, and embraced the practice of meditation. She serves on its board and is actively involved in the activities at the Center. During her healing she spent weeks in silent retreats, a practice she continues.

"Meditation really made a huge difference to me. I was looking anywhere for rescue and direction. At last I was able to let go of the therapists and grief groups. Through it all I have come to more congruency and clarity. As you know, the doctors said I would never walk again. In my mind I just knew I had to get up and get going. I was not going to be confined to a wheelchair for the rest of my life. I declared that I would ski by the millennium and I did.

"I come from a pretty strong line of women. My mother kind of just charged through life. She divorced my father, something that wasn't done at the time, and moved us to New York City from the Midwest. She was head of the drive for war bonds during the Second World War, spoke all over the country, was president of the Junior League.

She was a very tall, commanding person, and I always felt that I had to do the proper thing because of her. I was very driven as a younger woman. I had to achieve, be the best, be in charge, be president. But I never wanted to fit in a mold."

Sally has made a practice of doing the unexpected. World-traveled, on one trip she took her three sons on a tour of the Soviet Union as far as Siberia and down to Georgia before the area opened for tourists. While on this trip she saw the needs of Russian women and thus far has created three Lovett Women's Community Centers in a remote part of the Russian Far East where women work together for better education, employment, and contraception. She has been a professional volunteer most of her life and views this work as a regular job. She feels strongly about the value of the volunteer sector and started a department of the United Way in Ohio to establish respect for the work that is done. Currently Sally serves on a long list of boards and institutions.

"Unfortunately, I don't have a single passion, as I have so many interests. I enjoy weaving and have done a number of commissions. When I was at Spence and Vassar I studied music and theatre. I love to sing and would have enjoyed being on Broadway or in the opera. Opera singers make me cry because their instrument is from within. And then to learn the languages, act, coordinate with an orchestra, and remember it all. My mother took us to the opera when I was little, and I still love it.

"When I was a child I was left alone at home. I guess my parents thought I was old enough. I can still see myself sitting in the library in the corner of the sofa. We lived in a very deserted place, on an estate high on a wooded hill in Des Moines, Iowa. More than once my uncle came to the window and pretended to be a wolf. He thought he was being funny, but I was terrified. After that I could not stand to be alone. At this age and only in the last few months have I been able to spend the evening at home alone.

"Bob's presence is always here with me. In the evening while I am in the hot tub we have a conversation. Often this white heron shows up on my deck, and he stays for quite a long time. I was telling one of my sons about it. It's always when I've had some kind of moment of inner clarity, usually in connection with something that Bob would have identified for me."

These experiences hold great meaning for Sally, and it is clear that for her spirit and form are connected.

Veena Merchant came to the United States for the first time in the 1960s under the auspices of the Indian government. She was sent to manage Sona the Golden One, a boutique in New York City which showcased the textiles, handicraft, and clothing of India. She began slowly to create a new life for herself in what would become her adopted country. In India she had been editor-in-chief of a major fashion magazine and had owned the country's first modeling agency. Her women models were chaperoned to their assignments to reassure their parents. Striking, intense, a maverick and original thinker, she learned early in life to trust her instincts and put her thoughts into action. And while she might have felt the fear, she did it anyway.

Veena is now editor-in-chief of NEWS INDIA-TIMES and director of "Desi Talk," a political talk show for TV Asia sponsored by the Indian American Center for Political Awareness, of which she is a founding member. In the early seventies she became the deputy publisher of INDIA ABROAD. I remember accompanying her, because she was filled with trepidation, to meet its publisher and founder, Gopal Raju. It was then a fledgling newspaper but came to be known and respected worldwide for its excellence. I watched Veena through the years as she grew and flourished, moving from one new arena to another and learning everything she needed to know as she went.

Veena Merchant

"THE CHALLENGE WAS that I was never trained for any particular profession as such and I felt compromised many, many times. I spent the better part of my life as a young woman pretending to be a man in my work life because that is the only way I could be accepted. Now I can accept myself as being an intelligent, informed career woman, proud to be a woman, who understands her womanhood, her gender, and sincerely likes being a woman, and I want to stress that.

"The rewards of my career have been a feeling of independence and self-respect. My approach to the media early on was with feel-good stories, entertainment, but when you learn to deal with hard news, you become socially conscious. You begin to respect and understand the responsibility of the media, become conscious of doing the right thing, and realize that what we write about changes people's lives.

"One of the most poignant examples for me was, while on a flight, I heard a mother and daughter talking—the daughter was about ten and she was questioning her mother's judgment about some issue, and her way of authenticating her own view was to say, 'But Mom, the paper you read had an article that said x, y, z.' That really woke me up, and I saw how lives are impacted by the information in the media.

"We run matrimonial ads in the paper, as is the Indian custom. I was in Boston visiting my daughter—this was in the 1980s—it was a rainy day and I had to fax something to New York and we finally found this tiny shop that was open. When the owner found out I was from the paper he actually touched my feet. Needless to say, I was shocked and asked, 'What are you doing?' and he said, 'My daughter is so happy, she got married because of the matrimonial ads in your newspaper, we found her husband through those ads.' "

Inspired by Jane Fonda's programs, Veena pioneered aerobics in India with her television series on India's national television. The show changed the thinking of men and women about exercise as they discovered that it could be fun. Veena gave private classes for guests in major hotels and free classes for women who could not afford them. She unexpectedly became a major celebrity, mobbed by crowds seeking her autograph everywhere she went.

Recently on a trip to New York, where Veena still lives, we had the luxury of being able to spend some time together, and, like it is with old friends, we seemed to pick up our conversation without missing a beat. We met at her apartment on the Upper East Side. Her cozy home reflects her Indian heritage with images of Ganesh, the symbol of prosperity, and a quiet corner for reflection. I asked her what she wished she had known when she was younger.

"I wish I had been equipped with general life skills, that I had been clearer about my priorities, both emotional and financial. I never learned that it was a good idea to buy yourself a home or real estate or what kind of education pays off in terms of your career, and I couldn't impart those lessons to my daughter. My mom was such a young girl, younger than eighteen when I was born, and while she loved me, she didn't know how to be a mother, and my dad was an absentee dad, away all week.

"The emotional absence of my parents certainly had an affect upon me and may have had an affect upon the way I was with my own daughter. I had a different kind of childhood—we didn't go to school, we were taught at home—with a governess, and there was little socializing with others. We were brought up in a very austere, Victorian-thinking, restrained, aristocratic way.

"As a young girl I was reading books by Jane Austen—Emma was my heroine—but I was also reading about politics. My dad was very active in the movement for India's freedom and at one point made us throw out everything in our home that was British. He was a great supporter of Gandhi, who died about a year and a half after India became independent in 1947. My dad died several years later, leaving us without resources and on our own.

"When I met my husband I was still like a child in terms of the world, and in many ways he was more like a dad. So I would say that I grew up with him, but he was brought up in spoiled abundance, the very opposite of my life until that time. Sometimes two opposites make a good pair, and perhaps that was the attraction. When I came to the United States and stayed, I never thought of myself as separated from him. We never divorced, and until long after he died in India my mind would immediately go to call him to help me solve a problem.

"I could not think of myself as a widow. As you know it took a trip to India, my pilgrimage as I call it, to the places—the hospital, the place where his ashes resided—to feel his being around me and finally accept that he was gone. When we were together, it was the open sixties, and in that environment and for a person like me who never accepted openness emotionally, there was plenty of room for jealousy, and I discovered this aspect of my temperament. We were in a constant whirlwind, with an opulent social life, travel, and entertaining. My daughter was born during this time, and I know now that I was an absentee mother in the sense that she could be sitting in my lap and my mind was somewhere else, my own pain was so in the forefront that I dealt with it more than I dealt with her. She was a little girl when I came to the United States and I left her alone for one year—I have never forgiven myself for that, it was devastating for both of us. I sent her to boarding school and even now I get a feeling in the pit of my stomach when I think of the moment of my car turning around after leaving her, so the feeling of an empty nest came very early. I have learned so much from my daughter. Our conversations really opened my eyes to so many things. She has been more like a friend, and that perhaps has been my shortcoming as a mother. We have been able to work through many of our issues, and we speak every day. She is married now and I see the ways in which she is so wise in handling her own daughter."

Veena's daughter lives in the Midwest and while they see each other frequently, she says the sound of her daughter's voice every morning lights her up, and hearing her granddaughter makes her feel joyous. Our conversation continued to weave its way through many themes, intimacy, age, beauty, growth, and change.

"South Asian women, when we first come here, find the lack of respect towards older people frightening, as elders are honored in India. You would never think in terms of not giving that person a seat or interrupting them when they were speaking. I had never heard of age discrimination, and thought this must be some mistake, some misunderstanding. Being sixty is thought of differently in India, where life expectancy is not as high as in the United States. For me, being in my sixties is still mid-life, it's a matter of keeping my physical and mental agility. I never had an aging crisis, because as much as I'm American in the democratic spirit, I'm not American in this way. Here things gravitate around youth, feeling and looking good, especially in the consumeristic way the media presents the message. I didn't pay attention to my age until I was sixty, but as I have become aware of it, I find that it is straightening out my priorities. There is not enough time to do all the things you want to do, and you note the things you need to do more quickly.

"I don't remember what age it was—one fine day I knew that not every man I met was going to be turning around saying 'Wow,' and I had to let go of the fact that I thought I was a damn sexy woman. I could no longer rely on my looks. However intelligent or deep thinking you are, this society makes thing easier when you are good looking. I realized that I must further develop my intellectual prowess.

"I have always had a very strong sense of spirituality, an extremely strong sense of my intuitive thinking, my instincts. I have always lived by them. As I grow older, those things grow stronger. I feel that I understand life better and I feel my spirituality more deeply. I have always given myself permission to do what I want. Let's say that at this point there is not much to lose, there is a shorter span of life left, so I want to embrace what gives me pleasure and joy with much more urgency than I've ever felt. I realize that unless you share with a partner there is a major part of emotional life that is not lived. I wish that I could catch up on that somehow, the physical intimacy, to wake up in the morning and have a cup of coffee with someone who shares the same home, go to the opera, theatre, then discuss it. These things are so important and I'm afraid I'm missing them."

I asked Veena what makes us sensuous and vibrant as we grow in age.

"That's a really interesting question. I'd like to pretend that I'm a man and say what I would like in a woman. To me, sensuality is all about feeling your essence as a woman, being pleased, delighted, proud, and liking who you are. So as I grow older I'm more definitely a woman. I lived for the longest time pretending to be a man in my work life. Age gives you the time to grow into yourself, to have a better understanding of who you are, and feeling secure within creates an aura of vibrance and vitality."

Veena and I talked about the situation in the world, agreeing that we are at a crucial moment and that women's and children's lives are the most affected. Veena constantly reports on the issues and queries how, collectively and individually, women can make a difference.

"What is happening everywhere in the world is horrible. I am an international human being. I have lived in other countries, but America is still the best. We are a superpower and as a functionally good democracy can make change in the world, but we must make changes in this country toward non-violence and race-free thinking. Unless we change in America, how can we ask the world to change?

"Indian Americans have had economic success, but we are not very politically connected. With 9-11, we've had so much backlash because of mistaken identities it has made me more aware of the racial problems and attitudes in this country. 9-11 gave people license to look over their shoulder and say, 'Oh, so and so is colored and could be a terrorist.' Fear brings out a lot of underlying attitudes, and race is such a universal issue. I feel creatively and intellectually challenged by these issues and want to write more about them. In fact, I'm thinking of introducing a column from the Indian American Center for Political Awareness that will discuss these things.

"Women represent over 50 percent of the world's population, and yet we are described as a minority. I think this world needs a plural message, all of us getting together and spreading the message of love and non-violence. Millions of individual messages are what makes public opinion, and public opinion changes the world. We need to verbalize our thoughts, write a letter to a congressman, to a lawmaker. We are so busy in our everyday rush that we tend to bury these thoughts.

"Our individual voices make up the world, and we can make a difference if we verbalize, vocalize, and express ourselves on crucial issues."

As I step through the door of her home tucked into a flower-filled cul de sac overlooking the San Francisco Bay from Sausalito, I am immediately struck by Olga Murray's joyful presence. Her face breaks into an impish grin that draws me in, her eyes sparkle with life and curiosity, and I sense a heart brimming with kindness. As a young girl Olga developed a wanderlust that has taken her around the world, but she truly lost her heart in Nepal. In the late 1980s this love developed into a second career.

Olga Murray

"I WAS BORN IN TRANSYLVANIA, which is now Romania. I'm Hungarian. I came to New York with my mother when I was six. My father had come four years earlier and set up a business. I graduated from high school in 1941 when I was sixteen, one month after Pearl Harbor, and I left home and came to California. I still remember my mother crying when we said goodbye at Grand Central Station. When I was in grade school, one of the girls told about Trinidad during show-and-tell, and as she was describing it, I thought, I must go there! I have to see this place. My family teased me about it for years. They used to call me "Trinidad." I had this yearning, I wanted to see and do things.

"I had parents who adored each other, a loving and supportive family. When I was sixteen I asked my mother if I was beautiful, and she thought for a moment, and then she said, 'Yes, Olga, you are beautiful, but you don't know it. Do you have any idea how your eyes shine, how smooth your skin is, how thick and beautiful your hair is? You are slender and shapely. Your hands are so lovely. You have no idea how beautiful you are.'

"From my father I got the idea that I could accomplish anything, no limit. I just had to work hard and want it badly enough. My father was funny, charming, and good natured, a character. He believed everything good was going to happen in his life, and it did. This was such a gift. I didn't realize it till later as I saw people with defeatist attitudes. He was apprenticed to a furniture maker in Hungary in his childhood, and he was a fine craftsman. We were very poor during the Depression, but we had a happy family life, and eventually he had a shop in New York City and made furniture for very wealthy people like the Rockefellers. He learned English by reading The New York Times every day. I learned from him that it doesn't matter how much money you have, what matters is the kind of person you are. Culture was very important to him. He was a cello player, he read, he loved art, and he became an avid photographer. New York was filled with artists at the time, and many were his friends. He told me that in the 1930s Georgia O'Keeffe wanted to exchange one of her paintings for one of his chairs, and he told her no because he didn't like her work! I couldn't believe it!

"I moved around quite a bit during the war—I lived in Kansas City, Los Angeles, Indianapolis, and Denver. I always got a job.

"When I was working at the army hospital in Denver I met a woman who suggested that I go to college. It had never occurred to me, as nobody I knew went to college, but I thought, That's what I'm going to do—I'm going to go to college! I went back home, took the entrance exams for Columbia University, and went there for a year and a half. I realized that I wanted to have the experience of college life on a campus, so for a period of time I went to a small college in Ohio. I returned to Columbia and got a degree in Political Science. I applied to work for the State Department, thinking it was a way I could travel. I was turned down. This was the first failure of my life.

"So I went to Washington to find out why. I found out they had all kinds of information about me, and I was turned down because I still had relatives in Iron Curtain countries and my mother had signed some petitions on the street for something or other. It was during the McCarthy era.

"While I was in Washington, I heard there was an opening for a job with Drew

Pearson. Well, I got the job, and I was so excited that when he told me what he was going to pay me, I said, 'I'll work for less!' It was wonderful. I answered his fan mail—buckets and buckets came in every day. Some were threats, some were about politics, some were from kids, and lots were from people asking for help. I had permission to sign his name and carte blanche to call any department in the government. He was a very feared man in Washington, one of the few who dared to attack McCarthy. Our phones were tapped all the time.

"It was fascinating, but after a few years I realized it wasn't a career, and I decided to go to law school. At that time many law schools would not admit women. I applied to George Washington University and was accepted, and Mr. Pearson let me keep my job and work around my classes. I did research for him and had sort of my own little department. This was during the Korean War. Soldiers would write with complaints about the military, and I would call the Pentagon. Mr. Pearson had a weekly column that I would write.

"So I graduated, passed the bar exam, and came to San Francisco because the man I was in love with was here, and we were married a year later. I never should have married him, but what did I know?

"He was fascinating, brilliant and neurotic, and had a great sense of humor. A great big rugged outdoorsman, climber, sailor, skier, backpacker, doing all these things I had never done. It was just fascinating. We divorced after six years, but it was a failed divorce because we stayed close after that. He went up to Alaska to fish but would come down here and we lived together. We got along much better when we weren't married, but he died quite young. He was crazy about his children, who were ten and twelve when we married. Those children and I just fell in love with each other, and we're still very, very close. I have two grandchildren. My oldest grandchild came out to Nepal as a volunteer for eight months.

"At that time it was very difficult for a woman lawyer to find a job, there were so few of us. I was really scared, but I got the first job I applied for, at the California Supreme Court. That came about because I had broken my ankle trying to learn to ski, and the distance to the court was a far as I could manage on crutches. I think I got the job because Chief Justice Phil Gibson was a closet liberal, and I had worked for Drew Pearson. When he retired I continued working for Chief Justice Stanley Mosk. I was there for thirty-seven years as a research attorney, and it was the most satisfying, intellectually stimulating job in the world. I was able to help write important decisions in the areas of civil rights, women's rights, and environmental policy."

I had sent Olga the questions that set the framework of our conversation and, as she is a great raconteur, things flowed effortlessly. It was easy to see how she had become "Olga Didi," which means "older sister Olga," to the children of Nepal. We were cozied up in a corner of her bedroom to talk, with a breathtaking panoramic view of San Francisco Bay filling the window. This view also greets you as you enter Olga's home, and if you were to bathe in her deep tub you would see it filling the floor-to-ceiling window and reflecting in a mirror of the same size. Asking Olga about her adventures led to a series of wonderful stories about the life she lives now.

"I've had a lot of adventures over the years, traveling to India, all over Asia, and to Africa. I was almost sixty the first time I went to Nepal. I love to hike and I understood that people go trekking there, so I decided to go. As I was going through the airport I just felt comfortable, and I loved the look of the people on the street. The children were dressed in rags, they were all hungry, they had no toys to play with, and yet they were all so happy, so filled with joy. Much more so than the average American kid. And they all wanted to go to school! So I said to myself, All right, I know now what I'm going to do with the rest of my life.

"I always knew that when I retired I would work with children. If I go to a cocktail party and there's a hundred adults and three children, I'll be with the kids. I found out through a volunteer English teacher at an orphanage that I could give scholarships for these kids to go to college. So I gave five scholarships, and once back in the States I was constantly after my friends to do the same, and this went on for a couple of years.

"In 1987, I went back with a bunch of friends on another trek. We were in this remote area—most of Nepal has no roads and no electricity—and I broke my ankle. I didn't know it was broken, but I couldn't put weight on it. My friends wanted to go back but I said, 'No, no, we traveled 10,000 miles to get here.' For the next eight days I was carried on the back of a porter. My sherpa knew exactly what to do. He filled a carrying basket with sleeping bags and a mattress, gave me an umbrella, and I saw everything backwards for eight days. I said to myself, One of two things has to happen—I'm either going to have a nervous breakdown or I'm going to enjoy this. Nothing in between.

"So there I was, being carried on the backs of these four wonderful people whom I had never seen before, each taking a turn, over bridges with many planks missing 200 feet over a roaring river or along a ledge with the basket dangling over a 3,000-foot drop as the porter made a turn. It was great, though. I just decided to trust them, and, you know, I wasn't in any pain. As this one little guy—he was smaller than me—was huffing and puffing, oh God, how I wanted to levitate! The doctor who set my leg had just opened this hospital for orthopedically disabled children. I got involved and now we have a big program there."

Whew! As one who is not comfortable with heights I was trying to imagine this experience, and I said to Olga that this had to be one major life lesson in trust and letting go of fear. She pulled out her Nepal scrapbook to show me photos from the perilous journey, of the orphanage, and of all the children celebrating her eightieth birthday. The photos of children arriving emaciated at the orphanage and looking healthy and happy only five weeks later is a testament to Olga's impact.

"In 1990 we officially formed the Nepalese Youth Opportunity Foundation, NYOF, and in 1992 I retired to work full time with the foundation, living six months here and six months in Nepal. I could never have done this without the support of Justice Mosk. He was proud of what I was doing and allowed me to spend huge amounts of time in Nepal before I retired.

"Two principles have been the major guides of my life. One is justice and the other is kindness. If I had to choose one over the other, it would be kindness. As I have gotten older I think I've been able to follow those principles with more bravery. We have such abundance here. When I see all the teaching materials and toys in our kindergartens and think of a typical Nepalese village school where children sit on a hard bench all day with nothing to eat—and then hear complaints from Americans about things that shouldn't matter—I feel really bad about the injustice of it. In Nepal people are so poor only 15 percent of the country has electricity. Half the children under five are undernourished. There has been this terrible war. Tourism and carpet making have disappeared with the insurgency that certainly had a just cause initially but became very brutal. The corruption of the government, the squandering of foreign aid, the king declaring himself a monarch and stripping power from the government—

"There have been huge demonstrations. The day I left to come here, the king announced that he would reinstate parliament, and the country changed overnight. People ran out into the streets in their pajamas cheering with excitement. I hated to leave."

Olga's foundation has created a nutritional rehabilitation center and children's homes, and has provided schooling and scholarships that make a huge difference in the lives of the children, but among the projects that most touched my heart was the program for "indentured daughters."

"There is an area in Nepal called Dang with an indigenous group where a custom is prevalent among the very poor large families who have no land and whose average income is around $200 a year. The fathers sell their daughters—seven, eight, nine years old—who have never been away from home, don't speak the language, into servitude to these labor contractors who come to an annual festival. They haul them into buses and place them as servants in homes and teahouses in Katmandu, where their lives are at the whim of their employers. Many are sexually abused, beaten, not even given decent food. The fathers are paid $50 a year.

"We found out about the practice from our executive director and with his help we were able to create a program that helped these families become more self sufficient. Each family was given a piglet they could breed or sell, which would bring them income. We started a vast propaganda program against the indenture practice. When the girls came back at the end of the year, we put them in school. We had street plays that the girls wrote and performed about their suffering. We started with thirty-two girls, and in six years over 2,500 girls have been through our program. We have completely wiped out the practice in the areas we targeted. A big international agency heard about what we are doing and came in and helped. We got the mothers into an income generating program so that they could help pay for the girls' schooling. These girls, who were like slaves, have become so empowered that if their fathers make such a suggestion they will tell the father no, that it's illegal, and they won't go. For the girls fourteen, fifteen years old we have started a vocational program where they are learning to sew, and now we have 2,500 girls who need uniforms, so they have a ready market. My goal is to see the practice of indenturing daughters eradicated in Nepal.

"We have so many programs going on now, including one for the untouchables or Dalit population. If you believe in instant gratification, Nepal is the place to be.

"The advice I give to young people who are going through hardships is this: I guarantee them that when they get through this terrible time, while they may not realize it now, they will be strong, able to meet the challenges of life in ways they never could have before. So they can't lose!

"One of the great pleasures of being older is being able to be unconventional and unselfconscious. A couple of years ago I was invited to a very elegant birthday bash in St. Petersburg, Russia, by a very wealthy man who just took over the town, flying people in from all over Europe. The night before I was to go, I woke up with this huge bloody gash on my nose. I had slept on the zipper of my pillow. My first thought was What will all of those elegant people think of me? I quickly realized they wouldn't care about my nose, they would just think of me as a person. Then I thought, Isn't it great to be eighty! If I were twenty-five, I would have died of humiliation. But I just covered it up the best I could and had a wonderful time. It was a terrific event, but I kept thinking about the millions it must have cost and what I could have done with that money for the kids!"

Daphne Muse and I are comfortably settled in one of the studios at her home in Oakland, California, a room filled with an organized collection of artifacts, memories, and works in progress. Among the many photographs of family and friends, I am struck by one of her favorite aunt. A dried flower corsage is pressed under the glass in homage to her memory. A row of miniature chairs holds a collection of dolls, many of them made by her mother, a fine textile artist who has sewn everything the dolls wear from their underwear to their shoes.

Along one wall is a Japanese tansu chest, its surface covered with a collection of woven African baskets, its drawers filled with jewelry designed by Daphne from beads and other ephemera she has collected over the years. The worktable is awash in trays of necklaces, all works in progress, and another small chest is filled with things waiting so be fashioned into existence by Daphne's fertile imagination. Hanging from Japanese kimono poles are magnificent kimonos and African robe-like coats designed by her mother. The creative energy in the room is palpable.

Daphne Muse

I have known Daphne for more than twenty-five years. She was among the first friends I made when I moved to California in the late 1970s. She is a woman of African American and Cherokee descent who has a way with words that has led to many shared moments of side-splitting, tears-running-down-your-cheeks laughter. She is a writer, social commentator, editor, and archival consultant working with institutions and private individuals on collections and acquisitions. Recently she was named director of the Women's Leadership Institute at Mills College, Oakland, California. Although she is currently working on children's books number five and six simultaneously, her southern temperament influences her way of getting things done.

"I NEVER THINK OF WHAT I DO AS A CAREER. It's my life's work. I am never busy because 'busy' makes my heart hurt. I don't do busy, I am simply tending to the demands of the day for my life's work."

Daphne is an energy to be reckoned with when it comes to speaking and writing her mind. She is honed by years of political activism in the civil rights movement that started with Brown vs. Board of Education.

"I entered the tenth grade in Washington, D.C., about 1959, in a school that was predominantly white. As soon as the black students arrived, white students fled. The experience made me feel horrible—we couldn't understand it. They didn't even know us individually. But I had a history to tie it back to, as my parents spoke very openly about their experiences in the workplace. Most of the white teachers stayed, and some of them were very good. In the twelfth grade, my friend Esther and I—Esther's father was a diplomat from Ethiopia—went with a group of others to testify before Congress about the appalling conditions in the district schools. But there were other things about high school that were wonderful. Being the only girl in a family with four brothers, I loved sports. I ran track, played volleyball and tennis. My father gave me my first tennis racket."

When Daphne graduated from Fisk University she began teaching as well as working at the Drum and Spear Bookstore in Washington, D.C., which served as a meeting place for political organizing and intellectual exchange. There she met some of the most stimulating writers and activists in the front line for civil rights.

"I learned to dream as never before—it was so powerful, the intersection of the women's movement and civil rights. Black women were redefining themselves and discovering all the great women who had come before them. I was meeting so many historians and black writers, like Gwendolyn Brooks, Toni Morrison. I was traveling to the Caribbean for the bookstore, finding books for them to publish. Drum and Spear also published my first book. It was a collaborative effort, called *Children of Africa,* a book for children and parents, and it's still in print.

"The book I'm currently working on is *The Rosa Parks Secret,* about the time that Parks stayed at our home in 1980. My daughter, who was seven, had to keep the visit a secret. Ms. Parks didn't want to be inundated by the media, and she didn't enjoy hotels. I was working on a project to honor graduates, including Rosa Parks, and the Highlander Civil Rights School that taught people non-violent tactics and movement strategies. Rosa Parks didn't simply say, 'My feet are tired,' and refuse to give up her seat that day, but for various reasons the real stories get repressed. About the third day she was with us, when my daughter was on her way to school, a button popped off her dress, a dress my mother had made for her. Ms. Parks, who was a great seamstress, sewed that button back on. I just burst into tears, it was such touching moment.

"My earliest memory of my mother's sewing is a lavender dress that she made for me when I was eleven years old. I will never forget it because I wore it to lunch with this friend who came to take me out, as my mother was too busy raising five children and dealing with a difficult marriage.

"With the birth of my daughter, the relationship between my mother and me changed, and over the years, as we have gotten older, we have enjoyed a great friendship and many interests together—museums, music, shopping, restaurants, antiquing—and I feel tremendously privileged to have watched my parents grow up. I've seen my mother grow to an elder, thriving in her life as a textile artist and a fully independent woman.

"I was very close to my father growing up. There was an ease in the way I could relate to him that I didn't experience with my mother. He was the one who sat me down one summer evening in July and went through this whole biology lesson about my period. I don't know what I would have done if not for him, because in sixth grade I don't even remember people whispering the word 'period.' My mother just could not handle that kind of conversation."

I asked Daphne about her own experience of parenting and what she learned from the experience.

"It was clear to me that I wanted to become a parent, but it was so much more difficult than I thought it was going to be. Practical things I could do well—the emotional things were very hard. The constant demand to give and nurture, I wasn't prepared for that. I knew how to be with boys, having had so much responsibility for my brothers, but it's very different raising a girl. I didn't even know how to do Anya's hair, and there is something so primal about being able to take care of your daughter's hair. I worked too hard at trying to be my child's friend and not her mother, and I learned that that's asking too much of a child. Being a parent taught me patience, a hard lesson with my temperament. But it has carried over into my creative life; you can't force a poem, a novel, or a story when it ain't ready to be born—and trying to force it makes you insecure. You cannot build a life on insecurity. I had to learn that when you use your insecurities to shape yourself, you can really do a lot of things that destroy your spirit. For a while I did that to myself, especially by comparing myself with other artists and writers. I was supporting their work, and often I felt I would never measure up.

"But now I'm at a point where I feel so whole, and I am so pleased to be Daphne Muse. Every failure, every challenge, every victory, and many of my dreams have come to make me who I am, and I am grateful for that. I have revisited some of those old failures and challenges, flipped them over and used them as stepping-stones to claiming all of myself. I learned that I am a product of the society that constructed me, also my parents, my ancestors, and all the history that goes with that. I find that I have these primal ancestral callings where I find myself doing things, especially in my garden. There are days when I absolutely have to stop everything I'm doing and plant. I remember my Aunt Sadie, who took the tragedy in her life and started a garden. That's how I started my garden. Whenever someone I care about is killed or dies, somebody or something I want to acknowledge, I plant. It feels like something my ancestors did thousands of years ago."

I asked Daphne what she felt about being over sixty.

"On my sixtieth birthday, I swam sixty laps.

"I was clear that I was not going to be a Sears and Roebucks sixty-year-old. I remember women wearing the dowdiest clothes, bemoaning aging. But I never saw my mother do that, and I liked the gracious way in which she and many of the women I am surrounded by have embraced aging. It's not the bane of our existence, but something that is honored, respected, and celebrated, despite whatever nicks, dings, and bangs we're dealing with.

"I am disturbed by the commercialism and the vanity that people choke on to keep from aging. It keeps us from growing into the glory and beauty of self and supporting that in the healthiest ways possible. The character that comes with a face that shows experience and a spirit that exudes that experience, that demeanor says, 'I've lived this life.' Every molecule in me has lived this life, and I have stories for every molecule. Some of which I can't tell!"

I laughed at the thought of Daphne being a Sears and Roebuck lady, as today her toenails are painted turquoise to contrast with her lime-green sandals and dress. I asked her about her thoughts about love and romance at this stage in life.

"I am living my love story. At first I didn't I didn't know it, because of this notion that I had or other people create, about what that looks like. A wise friend of mine said to me early on in my relationship with David that you never know how your package is going to come wrapped. Well, I'm having a ball unwrapping it to this day. Though that doesn't mean that there aren't days that I don't want to push him out of that wheelchair and he doesn't want to roll over me. We have been together for twenty-five years and married for nineteen. It's been marvelous to be in a relationship with someone who has such a sense of humor. You look at David and you expect one thing, but he is so different from how he looks. We share many things in common, but we're also very different. He's very linear, and I'm not. We share political passions, and he has taught me a lot about expressing my own passion and love. He's the best partner I've had, intimately and intellectually. We talk about a range of things, from math to marriage to racism to cooking, so many things, and he's multidimensional in his thinking. It's been a wonderful relationship, even when we're challenged."

"What makes women vibrant and sensuous as we age?" I asked Daphne.

"Having had that experience as a young woman, having had it well, and continuing to desire it. I still have moments when I feel just the awe of life. Seeing a flower bloom, that feeling you get when you have had the most deeply intimate moment and are talking with one another afterwards, that afterglow. Being with someone you riff with so fabulously intellectually, somebody who can laugh at your stupid stuff without making you feeling insecure and vice versa."

"We have talked about many things that bring you joy and light you up. Anything else that makes you sparkle?"

"Well, the faces of my grandchildren. They don't even have to say a word. The lineage continues the spirit of who I am, although they're very different people. Seeing people really live life to the fullest. We should be talking more about how to be the best person you can, how to embrace and live this life in such a way that you can become absolutely the most fantastic, fulfilled, realized person that you can be. When I leave this place, I want to go out on a good note, feeling that I did what I could to leave the world with something good, although I'm not leaving it good."

With penetrating eyes that seem to absorb everything, a romantically smoky German accent, and a sensual air of indolence about her, Beate Prilio is a woman with a magnetizing feminine force. From the time she was a little girl growing up on a farm deep in the German countryside, where she was sequestered at the end of the Second World War, she knew that she was a free spirit. She was a dreamer, a wanderer, an observer, unfettered as the birds she watched as she lay in the fields, free to soar in her imagination. Her mother fled a destroyed Frankfurt in the ninth month of her pregnancy to the safety of relatives living in a small country village. She nearly gave birth on the train, and was rescued by relatives who came to fetch her by horse and buggy. Beate spent her childhood with her mother's nanny and nine eccentric, unmarried, distant aunts who ran a large working farm, as the men were off in the war. Knowing that her child would not starve, her mother left before she was a year old to try to build a new life for them.

Beate Prilio

"MY CHILDHOOD WAS NOT AN UNHAPPY ONE, but I knew that I was a foreigner, a stranger to that place. I wanted my mommy, and she was not there. I had a romantic and glorified concept of her, but I had no idea about a father because there were no men. There was one man around when I was very little, and he died, so I lived only with women, all who were very nice to me. I would take a basket filled with bread, cheese, and fruit to the women working in the fields, talk to the cows, feed the baby pigs, go in the stable, gather the eggs, and churn the butter, always dreaming up a storm and enjoying my own little world.

"I met my father for the first time when I was six years old. He had a huge beard, had been a prisoner of war, and was very traumatized. When I saw him, I screamed in fear, and his first deed was spanking my bottom because I screamed. Our relationship was instantly clear. At that moment I knew he would never control me.

"My mother was in a convent when she was young and felt that would be perfect for me. I thought I was going to die there. Suddenly I was in a completely disciplined environment with the nuns, silent study time, and sleeping in a big room with twenty other girls. God did not talk to me—that was my big drama. What a sinner

I must be! Something was not right with me, and on my knees in that ice cold room, a rope wrapped around my waist, I did penance and prayed that it would change.

"For seven years the teachers tried to break my spirit. I had many, many, many hours with the principal and the mother of the school, but I was like a rubber wall.

"I was reading so many things, so much about romantic love, and when I finally got out of there I met a beautiful boy, became pregnant, and got married. I had some kind of syrupy idea of what marriage was and no understanding of what it meant to be a wife—we were both children. In the early sixties we became the ultimate dressed-up hippies, traveling with our daughter to India, Bali, Indonesia—we were part of that international traveling band. My first husband bought a house in Goa, and though we had our difficulties, we have remained friends. We both have a love of art, and I have continued to spend time there until recently when the house was sold.

"I was intellectually influenced by the Frankfurt School, a group of important thinkers—Theodor Adorno, Herbert Marcuse, Max Horkheimer, Walter Benjamin—who were employed by the Institute for Social Research at the Johann Wolfgang von Goethe University.

"Frankfurt was a rebel city, which appealed to my nature, with student revolts and demonstrations against the Vietnam War and for women's rights. I apprenticed for three years with a traditional master bookbinder and learned bookmaking by hand. When I moved to San Francisco, I also studied traditional painting at the Art Institute, but I gave up it up for public art, working with Polaroids and copy machines. I felt that everything that could be done with traditional art had been done. I wanted to explore something new.

"In my first marriage, I drove my husband mad with, from his point of view, my inactivity. He is a reckless doer and I am a reckless thinker, so even if I appear to be completely passive my head is going all the time. At one point he bought me a little antique shop. 'No, no I don't want it,' I said. 'Yes, yes, you will like it,' —and of course it was a complete failure.

"I did know, very, very early in my life, that I was a person who needed to be taken care of, and I laid my life out that way. I was very clear about it. Most women of my generation were eager to have a career, but I knew I could not handle that—it would restrict me completely. To be in an office, have a schedule that I would have to keep—no, no, I am free spirit!

"It was very difficult with my peers, who thought I was crazy. I did not want to be kept, but I did not want to have a career. I said this to my second husband before we married. 'I will never make money. I will never have a career. But I am not a stay-at-home wife. I am a free spirit.' And he accepted that—it has never been an issue. I have never had a moment of guilt about it. I knew that I would be loyal wife, and I have very good grey eminence. By that I mean I am a very good background person. I am not involved in society, so I am able to check things out, observe with more objectivity, and give feedback.

"I also bring vibrancy and adventure to my husband's life with my travels. He likes Hyatts and comfort, and I travel to test the boundaries of myself. When I take my crazy trips it's to see what frightens me, when and how I use my intuition, my heart, my habits, how I behave. It shows me who I am. Before my mother died, she said that her life was not good, and that affected me deeply. I know that I don't want to be at the end of my life saying "I wish I had.'"

Beate traveled alone for months in Papua, New Guinea, living with headhunters, exploring the Sepik River by dugout canoe with three guides and locals from the area. She recorded her experience by taking photographs, making videos, collecting art, and creating an exhibition upon her return. She has spent time in Russia, Japan, and Egypt. She went on a pilgrimage to Tibet as a way of thanking a young Tibetan boy for saving her life in India. He rescued her, along with several friends who by Muslim standards were inappropriately dressed and were being assaulted by a group of men in Delhi. He appeared with a rickshaw and the women jumped in, slapping and beating off the men with their shoes.

She took the trip to Tibet in 1980, before tourism began in the country, traveling with a group on a difficult route through China to get there. But, like the bird that flies away, she likes to return when she is wet and cold to the comfort and stability of home, holding hands, taking walks, the sweet things, the simple enjoyment of life.

"For about two and a half years I was a guide for the guests of the office of the German Ministry of Foreign Affairs. The director was my best friend. I would not call it work—it was more a 'geisha' job, to make sure they had a memorable time. They came from all over the world, diplomats, bankers, politicians. Once I was assigned to guide a Tibetan high lama. We couldn't really communicate, so he sang and played for me, and I sang to him. I would translate, handle the money, take them to their appointments, to restaurants, the opera, whatever they wished to experience while they were visiting Germany. This is how I met my second husband. He was visiting from America."

Beate has been married to a very prominent politician for the past twenty-seven years. As a European woman with a different idea about living her life, she chose not to participate in the role of the American political wife. She has spent much time in introspection, observing her nature, and, as she says, using her life as living art piece. I asked her how growing in age had affected her choices. She spoke of her forties as powerful and exciting and her fifties as full of change.

"During my fifties I was involved with three deaths and births. I found that they were very similar. They both have raw pain—there is nothing refined, you cannot pretend, no politeness about it, it is just raw. It makes you humble, how you get here and how you go out. It makes you appreciate life very much.

"While I still traveled, I was more reflective. I thought about my philosophy, took inventory. When we think of ourselves, we like to think of what is good about us. Yes, we think about the bad things but they swim on the surface like the fat on a soup. When we get angry, we try to rationalize the anger, we get conflicted. And so for six months or so, I experimented. If I was angry or had bad feelings toward someone, I forced myself to acknowledge this and to think out the worst to find out how bad I could really be. I wanted to have a more complete picture of myself, to explore my dark side. This was very hard to do because we gloss over these feelings. I could see a murderer sitting somewhere inside me, all those thoughts and feelings that are suppressed. Maybe I couldn't murder, but I forced myself to delve deeply and wrote down what I could do to know this part of my character.

"When I reached my sixties, I thought, Who do I know who is sixty? Nothing happens at this age. This is neither a hot nor a cold age. I felt a loss of identity. I noticed that I had become a woman of the second look. It took a little while to get used to this. When I see my face, I am not unhappy about it—this is what I have worked for.

"Perhaps there is a sweet sentimentality about youth and beauty. I have confronted myself about this time in my life and its advantages. I think with age we radiate confidence. That is what makes us vibrant and sensuous. I am very bold now about how I look at men directly. I even comment the way they did to me when I was young. I feel very comfortable about this and find it amusing. I might comment to a stranger, 'God! You are beautiful!' It is wonderful to be able to do this.

"But lust is gone, and I feel liberated. It used to bother me that at times there could not be another thought in my head. Sex, the act of making love, is so revealing. When were are young we don't know the difference between lust and love. Youth lust is like gulping down a glass of vintage wine without tasting. With age, we develop more sensitivity and awareness. I tried to tell my daughter that sex gets better when you are older, when you know more about yourself. I also find that the experience of an intense conversation, whether it is with a man or a woman, gives me the feeling of being fulfilled, recognized, appreciated, and nurtured in my soul. In a way it can be as satisfying as an orgasm."

Beate has an art studio on the upper floor of her home where many works in progress are laid out. The windows frame perfect views of San Francisco Bay. Here she spends time with her binoculars looking for images she wishes to capture to combine with pictures she shoots from her television screen for her latest Polaroid collages, a series she calls "the reality show." She has done exhibitions for Polaroid in New York and Germany and recently won an art contest in Germany to do a billboard, the ultimate piece of public art.

"Now my eroticism, my intensity, my thought goes into my artwork, but I have never wanted to be famous—for the simple reason that it would hinder my free spirit. You are imprisoned when you are famous. I observed this even as a child, when I saw what famous people had to do to get there. It is very nice to have these exhibitions, they just happen to me. But no way did I ever want to be famous. It would hinder my being."

And with that, we head back downstairs into the dining room to enjoy the most exquisite petit fours that Beate has laid out in a lovely setting for afternoon tea. I find myself thinking about the unique patterns we develop, the choices we make, and the circumstances that create the tapestry of our lives.

Mimi Silbert is the muse, the founder, the brilliance, behind the Delancey Street Foundation, a residential education center where hard-core felons, substance abusers, and other lost souls can find their humanity and reconstruct their lives.

Mimi Silbert

Who is this small, fast-talking powerhouse of a woman, this ferocious lioness? This woman who is able to face down, mentally and emotionally, a part of society given up for lost and wrestle them back to life? For thirty-five years she has been committed to the process she began to develop in a little clinic she set up while getting her doctorate in criminology at Berkeley. She was also working as a prison psychologist at the time, and she realized that traditional therapy didn't work for people who are in prison. Everything they did was self-destructive. Their behavior had to change radically and quickly. The basic premise of the clinic was that anybody who came for help had to do something to help someone else.

Mimi met John Mahar, who had heard about the clinic. While his background was the polar opposite of hers—Mimi describes herself as a misfit in the good-girl world, John was a brilliant, charismatic eighth-grade dropout—they shared similar ideas and ultimately decided to work together. The first center opened in the heart of elegant Pacific Heights in San Francisco, California, initially much to the ire of its neighbors.

Mimi and I are in a meeting room in the block-square residential complex located on prime Embarcadero real estate that since 1990 has housed residents, a moving company, and a host of rent-paying tenants. It is the most beautiful place along the waterfront, and people constantly inquire about purchasing or renting to live there. Mimi says to them, "Oh, I'm sorry, but you haven't screwed your life up enough!"

The miracle of this place is that it was built from the ground up by the residents, and its living area, restaurants, and moving company all are run solely by them. There is no staff, salaries, funding, or cost to taxpayers. Everything is self-generated. No matter how often I'm at the restaurant, I am always moved by the young men and women in their crisp white shirts, all residents, tending to the guests. Regardless of how far down they have been, they have risen to the best in themselves through the hard work of the program. As I waited for Mimi earlier, her banquet manager came in to set up a repast for us to enjoy while we talked. A feeling of caring was in his every move as he set down Mimi's favorite cup and thoughtfully arranged the platters. Mimi and I have known each other for many years. After our usual hugs and greetings, I ask her about the most adventuresome thing she has done, and her preamble leads to an unusual story.

"I CAME FROM A LUSTY, LOVING IMMIGRANT FAMILY. My dad was a person of great love. When you were around him, he was able to reflect to you how wonderful you were—anyone who was around him, he found their strengths and loved them for it. I grew up with that love.

"Yiddish was my first language. My mother was born in Lithuania and went through seven pogroms. The whole family was separated many times. My father had similar experiences in Poland and Russia. For the first twelve years of my life we lived in a little flat in a multi-ethnic ghetto in Boston. My grandparents, aunts, uncles, all my family came, the idea being that everyone would help each other. My family had struggled so much to get to America and had succeeded, so I grew up with the idea that struggle was a good thing.

"Eventually we moved. My dad had a little drugstore, my mother kept the books, and after school I was the soda jerk. I was a secret misfit, more on the inside than the outside. My life had been made easy by the struggles of my family, so I felt that doing well in school was a small thing to give back. I have the deepest respect for people who are willing to struggle for values, for goodness, decency, and integrity.

"I've always been a little itchy and outraged, I will never have peace of mind. I was able to be a very independent-minded kid because I was standing on the shoulders of complete security and love, although at the time I thought it was smothering.

"So there I was, eventually, married to a wonderful guy in a happy, comfortable life with a perfect job, feeling how nice it was to do good, and I told my husband that what was missing for me was struggle. It took a few years, but as the ideas that John and I were working on at Delancey Street grew, I told my husband that I had to do this—I had to leave—and while he didn't like it, he understood that I was driven.

"Also, money made me uncomfortable, because I was brought up to almost admire the poor, and it took me a long time to understand there is no nobility in being poor. So I moved into Delancey Street, taking our twin sons with me when they were about two years old, and that's where they grew up. It wasn't the world they would've had if I hadn't chosen to do this. For me it was the right decision, but I think my kids suffered in ways they might not have, and they sacrificed a lot. They're in their late thirties now. Both have become lawyers doing good work, and they are the anchors of my life. They have also given me four incredible grandchildren.

"You asked me what I learned from having children. The fact is that I continue to learn from my children—they are the people I trust most when I am not sure about something. They were always wiser than I am and still are.

"At one point I couldn't resist looking at their college essays, the part where you write your autobiography—and, believe me, I was steeled for the worst. Both began with 'I had an odd upbringing' and told stories that showed they had learned to be loving human beings, giving, moral, ethical, caring, and compassionate. All the things you could've ever wanted, what we were aiming for with the residents, they got by example. They learned about taking risks, that failure is just a step on the way to success. Here they were living with these huge forty-year-old guys who were just learning to read and write, and they could appreciate both their struggles and accomplishments. They worked hand-in-hand with the residents on the construction project and in the restaurant and understood intuitively that there is no separation between people. The residents were as much their friends as were their schoolmates from the fifth and sixth grade. I just wept. All during those years I was waiting for them to rebel because that's what I'm good at, and it finally dawned on me that they had rebelled by being good.

"Here we teach that we need each other. Our people come in unbelievably racist, they're all in gangs by race and have sworn to kill other races. It's fascinating to me, because my parents were persecuted for being Jewish, and one of the big groups among white prisoners are the Nazis. They come in here with swastikas all over them. I remember a guy sitting down and saying to me that his life had been to find Jews and blacks and kill them. He said, 'What are you going to do to me when you know what I have done?' I looked at him and said, 'I'm going to do the worst thing I can possibly do. I'm going to forgive you.' And he just wept. I said, 'You are going to tell me every last thing, and you are going to be sorry for it, but we are here together and we need each other. This is our family and we can't be mad at each other. And we for sure can't kill each other. We're all we have.'

"It's been years of all these gangs killing each other based on what block they live on, what color, what group. One day I realized what I've recreated here is this close, old-fashioned, ethnic American family where everybody knows too much about each other—we're in each other's business all the time. Just like it was in my neighborhood growing up. I am a parent, bringing people up again who didn't learn how to make life work for them.

"We are a huge family. We don't have much money—we pool everything and take care of each other because we don't believe in hiring baby-sitters! Aside from helping people change, there is a point to prove. People who are considered the problem have within them everything that's needed to become the solution. In order to find your own strengths, there has to be the weight of responsibility and ownership on you.

"Our average resident is a third-generation serious drug addict, gang member, criminal, coming from many generations of poverty. They have grandmothers yelling at them to come back into the life. Hope is not something they understand—they are angry beyond caring and despair. They may say they want to change, but how? It's like asking them if they want to eat some food they've never heard of. And, God, it's so phenomenal to see the day, it always happens, that a resident says, "You know, I've been saying what you tell me to this guy you put me in charge of. Truth is I just didn't give a shit because I don't care about nobody. And today I ran into him, and all of a sudden I looked at him, and it meant I cared. That's the first I've cared about anybody.'

"That's when they start to hope they can be different, that they can be decent. Act as if you care, eventually you'll care. Go talk to the new people, help them, forget about yourself. It's all about A helps B, A gets better. B helps C, B gets better. Get out there and give, focus outside yourself. I'm always saying, 'You have to take the hardest thing for you and do and do it.' When I was working on the construction of the building and had to figure out mechanical problems, it was hell—and critical for me to do it. To take something I was bad at and conquer it enough to make it work and not be afraid to look stupid."

As Mimi continued to tell me stories of the residents' lives, I found myself stunned into silence from the intensity of it all. I asked her how she kept from constantly crying, and she responded that she wept all the time. She talked about having to practice her own philosophy while dealing with the painful loss of her father and John Mahar, which left her immobilized and numb.

"I was trying to be strong and hold it together, be positive, and as I was listening to someone's story, my feeling just came flooding back. I got up in front of everyone and said, 'This is everything I am feeling and I am not at my best, but you aren't at your best and I ask everything of you, so who the hell am I to think my pain is so special?' "

Our conversation about losing loved ones turned to growing in age and media interpretations of the subject.

"Recently I was talking to my sons about someone, and they said to me, 'How old is he, Mom?' And I said, 'He's our age.' And they said, 'Mom, you and we are not the same age.' And I was stunned for a moment, because when I talk to them I feel like we're the same age, but I guess it's true—my sons are younger than I am!

"I was very busy on my life's mission. My dad had been ill, and people my age were starting to talk about retirement. With the deaths of people who were so important in my life I realized that my independence relied on everybody else believing in me. Age had not meant much, but reaching sixty meant something. What I know now is that you have to experience something to know it—you have to live through it. I used to think being sixty meant maturity, accepting things, being reasonable, having more peace of mind, but those things will never happen for me. I was odd at twenty and will be odd at eighty. I don't understand the concept of retiring to do the things you want to do. It's about laughing and playing, loving everything you do. I love being on the precipice with this huge family and constantly figuring out new things, not knowing what I am going to need to know. I just feel so lucky to be living in a community that is a 'we.' There is no 'I' in any of our lives.

"You asked me about my image of myself at this stage of life. I remember my Mom saying, 'You're going out on a date—put on some lipstick,' and my saying, 'But he asked me out without my wearing lipstick and I refuse to wear it.' You know I wear no jewelry. I don't know how to put on makeup. I know how to take it off the residents when they have it caked on. But now as I'm getting older, I'm putting on lipstick, or I think maybe I ought to cut my hair. I actually look in the mirror and think, What is this neck? I'm not supposed to have this neck! So it took the media a very long time to reach somebody like me. For years I never gave a damn, then I did, and now I have come full circle not to give a damn. I have earned this neck screaming at the residents. This is my face, my height, and these are my thighs, and they will never get long and thin. Screw it! It's never been about that, and it would be absurd for it to be about that now."

Delancey Street expanded its reach, and for the past eight years has run a charter school for Juvenile Justice kids out on Treasure Island. Exposed to the same formula that worked for adults, the students learned an entire year of academics through a project-based curriculum that revolved around renovating the first building for their school and adding an additional 25,000 square feet. The students also run the only restaurant on the island. Graduates come back to help new students. They tell them, "I built this roof. I built this room. I painted this wall." Needless to say, there is no graffiti here.

"We have five Delancey Streets around the country now," says Mimi, "and I can't do any more and keep that family feeling. But we have been inundated with requests from all over the world, so I finally decided to try to teach the model to other people.

"It takes a long time. I have based it on what I call the 1950s dating model—the slow dating process. We get to know each other and can part company before we get too far along. If we think they are going to 'get it' after a lot of travel back and forth we get 'pinned.' If that goes okay, we get engaged, and if all goes well we ultimately get married! We have many states and countries in various stages, but we have married with Virginia, Alaska, Hawaii, Singapore, lots and lots of places, some faith-based, some business organizations.

"I am trying to teach it from all angles, although each organization has a residential facility. In fact, a wonderful developer used our basic principles to build an entire community, and they did phenomenal things. The replications cannot use our name, but after they complete our program they are awarded a letter indicating that they are a replication of the Delancey Street Foundation."

Thousands of lives have been turned around due to the efforts of Delancey Street. With passion, caring, and commitment it's incredible what a difference one person can make. No doubt about it, Mimi Silbert will leave this world a better place for her efforts.

In her crisp white lab coat, stethoscope around her neck, Alyce Bezman Tarcher, M.D. exudes professionalism. She has been a doctor of internal medicine for more than forty years. To the delight of her patients, other aspects of her personality are also apparent. You notice that she is wearing a bright red belt, that her wrist is covered with wonderful ethnic bracelets, and that a black-and-white scarf accentuates her crisp white coat.

Alyce Bezman Tarcher

Alyce sparkles with energy and radiates empathy. She says that she isn't doing her job if she doesn't have 'a placebo effect' on her patients. She emphasizes the power of the body to heal itself and has the understanding to incorporate different methods to achieve this end. Believing that preventing disease is as important as treating it and that patients do better when they are involved with their own health, she may recommend doing tai chi or chi gong along with nutrition and stress reduction. With a background in research and biochemistry, she is well-versed in the strict discipline of science and brings the same analytical rigor to her practice of integrating alternate healing modalities, including traditional Chinese medicine, acupuncture, herbal treatments, and massage. Sometimes she even recommends chicken soup. She once wrote a prescription for it, telling her patient which restaurant to go to, and the restaurant owners wanted to display it in their window. She quickly recovered the prescription before this happened!

We are in the sitting room of Alyce's San Francisco home, a place filled with artifacts from more than four decades of world-wide travel and adventures with her late husband. Kilim carpets are scattered on the floor, and a grand piano fills a corner of the room. Everywhere, from the staircase to the living room, art and sculpture from Africa, Mexico, and Peru blends with the work of local artists and friends. Her beloved German shepherd, Isabella, a constant companion, is curled comfortably in her favorite spot on the sofa. A riot of color bursts through the windows from the garden. We settle in to talk and our conversation ranges over a broad number of topics.

"THE PRACTICE OF MEDICINE IS ESSENTIAL TO MY BEING, as I have always felt that I am a healer, but I love my home. I'm very much a homebody and especially enjoy sharing my home with good friends. I do my own gardening, except for the large pruning, and I like doing housework. I'm on my fourth German shepherd. I've had one since the beginning of my practice, when I used to make house calls in areas of the city that were marginal, and my husband insisted that I have a dog with me. I used to keep her in my office as well. An animal can have a very healing effect on patients. Years ago I had two elderly sisters as patients, and when one of them died, the remaining sister came to the office very distraught. I put her in the room with the dog, who sat there looking at her so intensely, as if he were listening, and she just poured her heart out. I was so touched by how much healing can be done with this kind of loving, nonverbal animal concern.

"It's unfortunate now that things are more formal, and it's no longer possible to have an animal in a medical office. Isabella is from two of my good friends who are breeders of world-class German shepherds. She gives me a great deal of comfort, especially since the recent death of my husband. Observing the behavior of my dogs has taught me how to maintain dignity in the face of illness and loss, how to age gracefully, and how to face adversity with composure."

Just as she was finishing her medical residency, Alyce met and married the man who was her soul mate and her scholarly, intellectual life partner, a man who was also a great deal of fun, loved her dearly, and with whom she enjoyed a life of adventure and a broad social network of good friends. I asked how she has coped with this new stage in her life.

"You are never prepared for the loss, but we are not given an invitation to life. The time comes when you understand that you have to make a nurturing environment for yourself. If you want to continue to be fulfilled, to have social contact, to not be invisible, you have to be proactive. You have to invite people over. And this is what I have done. It has made my life quite rich now in the face of being alone. I am very aware of how easy it would be to slip into a kind of void. You have to be mindful. I am not waiting for invitations, I'm extending them, having musicals and Sunday afternoon high teas in my home. It may be easier if you have a sense of your own identity. I love chamber music and have friends who play a variety of instruments. The anticipation, cooking, preparing for my friends is so enjoyable—it's always a wonderful time.

"Speaking of my husband, we had been at Oxford for a year, where I was doing a research project, and as he loved the sea he suggested that we take a freighter back to San Francisco. He was writing a book, and I had all the research I had just completed to write out. I thought that I would feel like a caged animal, but in a marriage there is compromise, so I agreed, and it turned out to be a very wonderful, romantic way to travel. We purchased pounds of books for the journey. We took a Dutch freighter from Amsterdam, through the Mediterranean, across the Indian Ocean, got caught in a few huge storms. I was called upon to tend to someone who had an accident during a storm. The captain asked me to his stateroom to see if we had to stop in Sri Lanka for help, reminding me that it would cost thousands to make this detour. I assured him this wasn't necessary, much to the disappointment of my husband, who always wanted to visit this country. So this was the beginning of our travels on freighters, banana and mail boats, to Finland, Alaska, the Orient, Costa Rica, Ecuador, Africa, Fiji, New Zealand. The quarters were often large and very comfortable. There was lots of time for reading and writing, and the people running the ships had great stories. You really get a close-up view of the culture of the countries you travel to that way that you would miss as a typical tourist.

"I also worked in Peru on a fully equipped hospital ship, Project Hope. The ship stayed for one year near the city of Trujillo, where I made medical rounds in the nearby hospital. I learned so much from the head doctor there, a brilliant clinician with little laboratory help but such finely honed clinical skills. Some of our Indian patients came many miles from their homes in the Andes Mountains. There was so much suffering, at times beyond our ability to change, as in some cases the diseases were too far advanced. Often expressing our interest and concern was our most important contribution. It was an intensely moving experience and certainly trivialized much of what we do and worry about at home. All of my travel has given me a greater understanding of people, and that has been of such value to me in my practice.

"In medical school I was one of two women in a class with ninety-two men. There were still relatively few women in the field. I was doing something that felt so natural to me and was excited beyond words to actually begin my studies. As you know, the desire to become a doctor arose in me during my childhood. One of the major influences in this decision was that my dear grandmother died suddenly of a stroke when I was five years old. I was aware of what had happened and felt very powerless. I decided that I never wanted to be in this terrible position again. It was a formative trauma at a very young age, and by the time I was eleven it was clear to me that this was my path.

"I am an only child, so I've always been accustomed to relying on my own resources. I was never around children as a child, and as an adult I wasn't at all interested in motherhood. I grew up in Omaha, Nebraska. My parents valued education but really left me to make my own decisions. I think if I had chosen to be a writer, teacher, or musician they would have felt it was fine as well.

"My grandfather had a farm where I spent many summers, and I loved it— bringing in the cows, riding the horses that pulled the alfalfa wagons, and finding where the hens had laid their eggs. Bringing the cows in for milking made it clear that you can't always have your own way. I had to learn to negotiate with Bossie, the cow in charge, because if she didn't move, those cows weren't moving either, and I would be in hot water.

"A part of me truly relates to the land and the farm and makes me sensitive to the importance of supporting the earth and its health. One of my patients came to the office suddenly and acutely ill. In talking to her about her recent activities, I found that she had been exposed to herbicides in her garden. This contributed to my concern about the dangers posed by toxic agents in our homes and the environment and their effect on human health. It led to the development of the book I edited and wrote on the subject in collaboration with a group of contributors, as there were no texts on the subject. Recently, with a small group close friends I went on a safari to Africa, and my interest in environmental medicine made this trip especially rich. It is a source of wonder—something quite unbelievable—to see the planet in its pristine state with flora and fauna, the wild creatures amid the wild places they inhabit, and it makes you realize that it is imperative to conserve these natural resources.

"At this point in my life, after such a rich and satisfying marriage, I wouldn't be interested in trying to have another relationship. I do have a coterie of male friends that we have known for many years. They have become an important part of my life, and I have dinner with them on a regular basis. This is very pleasant for me because all my life and work I've been around male energy. Gay men often enjoy friendships with women, and I certainly feel appreciated by them. It provides us an exchange of masculine and feminine energy that is not complicated by sexuality. There is a genuine warmth, interesting intellectual exchange, and we truly enjoy each other's company.

"Curiosity does not kill the cat. It keeps us alive, vibrant, and learning new things. The true meaning of old is when curiosity is gone."

The smell of rain informs the air on this misty March morning in San Francisco. Gazing out the window from the gracious dining room at the home of Glady Thacher, I notice that the trees lining the block have a soft, new, acid-green color, intense against a flat, colorless sky. One wall of the dining room is punctuated by a beautiful Japanese screen that appears to float in this light. A dining table that will accommodate meals for a big family and comfortable antique English Regency furniture complete the space. She has lived here since the 1950s, when her husband decided to move back to San Francisco from the East Coast to take over the family law firm.

Glady comes in from the kitchen carrying tea. There is a quiet radiance about this elegant woman who moves with the ease of one as comfortable on a hiking trail or tennis court as in a boardroom. Today she is dressed in gabardine trousers and a sweater in colors of lavender and sage, accented with a beautiful necklace of African beads from a local designer. Since the 1980s she has been engaged in the practice of Zen meditation and was honored recently by the San Francisco Zen Center as a community treasure for her long career in education, philanthropy, and social activism.

Glady Thacher

"I DIDN'T EXPECT TO GET MARRIED when I graduated from Smith—it was considered a wimpy thing to do, to slide from college into marriage. But I happened to get married. We didn't have much money, and my in-laws expected me to get a job. I was going to be a painter, but there were no jobs for painters. I was frantic looking for work and ended up at the Red Cross soliciting blood! I was so young—I believed that you had to know what you were going to do, and that the purpose of your life was set before you were thirty. Well, I have found that life is very long and has many changes. Transitions can be difficult, but they are the stepping-stones for growth and opportunity into uncharted areas. So much pressure is put on kids coming out of universities. There

is the idea that what you are going to be is determined by what kind of work you will do. When I talk to younger people, I want them to know there are many roads in life. That we can mess up one part of our lives and come out stronger.

"I was about twenty-one when I had my first child, and my second was born about twenty months later. I was still intensely involved in my art until I finally had to accept the fact that my mind could not be in my studio when I had to get the children to the pediatrician. The challenge emotionally was to wrest myself down from the ardent desire to be a painter, to be known in that way. A number of things converged. The paradigm I was working in, abstract impressionism, was hitting the wall. It was at a place where it had to burst out of the canvas. I knew that I would have to undress the image I had of myself, to close the door to my studio. It was a very fragile time losing that identity. It's difficult for people who would like to be the so-called artist, writer, composer, to dedicate their lives to their art, and it takes a tremendous amount of talent. I thought, I'll survive, even though I'm a nobody like everyone else, which I certainly didn't want to be! I began to do a little community work and then joined a board. I found that the same kind of energy was churning around, and I guess I realized that I wanted to emerge in my own way. That was a real no-no during the fifties, as women were supposed to be getting all the richness in life from their children and by supporting their husbands.

"I had given up painting, but eventually something else began to take hold in me. One thing led to another—the need for creative expression comes in many forms. So as my children were growing up, I began my first project, Enterprise for High School Students, a job placement program for students that I started in my living room. I had trained some women to be counselors, and kids were coming in off the street. I was listening to them, but I was not focusing on my own children, They would come in after school, and I would hear them say, 'Oh, Enterprise!' as they would go upstairs. My husband would come home and creep up the back stairs. There were desks, files, phones, copiers all over the living room, on the piano, everywhere. My desire to do things was so great that I didn't understand the impact it had on my family. I thought I was doing good work helping kids get jobs, but my own kids never took advantage of the service. I really had no idea about parenting.

"To complicate matters, it was the sixties, our oldest daughter was growing up, and, oh was that a challenge! I didn't know then the very simple and important fact that you need to love your children and not have ideas of who they have to be, that when you simply support and encourage them they'll give you much less trouble in the end.

I think you learn about parenting in hindsight unless you have a knack for it. These things I know now as a grandmother—I have ten grandchildren, and I lose my heart to them. They're so comical. I love how they just sit on the stone steps of the garden, just sit and look out."

Glady had a troubled and complicated childhood. She was born into an affluent and social Long Island family. When she was about eight years old, the family moved to gentleman-farm country in Old Chatham, New York, where the social set Glady's mother was part of enjoyed riding and hunting. They divided their time between there and Florida, as her mother was in the midst of a divorce.

"When I was about eleven and a half I was sent off to boarding school in the Berkshires, where I lived during the week, and following that, I went to the Shipley School as a full-time boarder. My summers were spent in Old Chatham. This period was a seminal time for me. My love of the country was deep and awakened my desire to be a painter. My education was isolating, and I lived in an interior world. If you have ever been on the old roads in the Berkshires in the wintertime, it's as if you are in a vacuum. My sister and I had a governess. My mother was married to her second husband, whom I disliked intensely, as he had an alcoholic personality, and our household began to get very complicated. My stepfather had three children. My grandmother had remarried and had a child, then both she and her second husband had died in the Depression, and her orphaned daughter came to live with us. Then my mother and stepfather had a child, and, thus, I had a young stepbrother. It was confusing, to say the least.

"I was very angry, shy, and jealous—there was a rivalry with my older sister. The anger fueled a sense of determination, and I took on a lot of physical risks, skiing, riding, being a daredevil and a tomboy and pitting myself against nature. Anger and jealousy are so destructive they're like poison. Later in life I had a wonderful mentor who said, 'Jealousy is as cold as a grave.' It really is. And shyness prevented me from understanding people.

"It wasn't until well on in my marriage, when I went to San Francisco State to get my master's in educational counseling, that I found myself able to relate to people, show my emotions, and it was a tremendous relief. All that had been in a locked box. I began to discover the richness of connecting when I learned to listen, drop my expectations, be vulnerable. It was this interchange with people that gave me the greatest nourishment—something I never expected at all. I had tried to find this nourishment in nature, but try as I might, the mountains would not speak directly to me.

"We're a part of the body of nature, but nature is not going to come in and bind our wounds and give us a sense of warmth and love. For me, it has come from friendships and the satisfaction of being in community services. Over the years, you develop these relationships, and I have found that they clothe you. I was able to bring parts of myself to infuse my community work and the development of Alumnae Resources, even though it was not painting. Looking back, I am able to see that it wasn't arbitrary, the relationships, the reciprocity, the give and take—all these things strengthened what I was doing."

Glady started Alumnae Resources in San Francisco in the late 1970s as a place for women who wanted to use their education, be taken seriously, and develop professional and managerial careers. There were women whose children had left the nest and were ready for a new stage as well as younger women looking for guidance. At the time, the glass ceiling was well in place. Consciousness-raising groups, National Organization for Women (NOW), and the struggle for women's rights were in full swing. Women were finally making inroads into the workforce in large numbers. The organization created a sisterhood, a place where women could be supported and gain new skills.

The organizations Glady has founded seem to follow her own path of development. At sixty, after serving as the founding director for the San Francisco Education Fund for a number of years, she felt she wanted to retire from the organization and was looking in another direction. She realized that both men and women her age were seeking a deeper meaning and purpose.

"My husband and I were backpacking with friends in the Sequoia National Park, and I happened to get over one of the passes before the others. It was at the Kings River area. I was used to having my breath taken away with exhilaration, but suddenly this vast landscape in front of me echoed a wakeup call that my life was limited and the space ahead was finite. It kicked up in me a strong feeling that I wanted to live a life that had integrity.

"The idea for LifePlan Center took hold. While I had not truly felt the impact of growing older, I knew that general attitudes about aging were having an effect on men and women. The feeling that we are sliding downhill, leftovers without status, that we should just retire somewhere, but not get sick and be on the government dole. There was no place to focus on the psychological, spiritual, and emotional things that are happening, and there was no description or expectation for this new time. It is up to us to chart this new territory. We all want to connect with something that gives us meaning, a sense of identity, and the confidence to live more truly to ourselves. The changes men have had to face, the idea of having to take their bags of skills and go from one thing to another, that was new. I celebrated that men were opening up, and we had a men's forum where they could get together for discussion. It's been a fascinating time these last three decades.

"As we grow older, there are things that need to drop away, as in nature the leaves drop off the trees, but it still can be a growth time. For me the practice at the Zen Center has been a way of bringing awareness, gratitude, kindness, and compassion into life. I have tremendous admiration for people who achieve something that is a real challenge, like getting out of a debilitating environment. I know that I have been fortunate as I did come from an affluent background and was able to have a good education. I have not had the experience of discrimination. When I ran the Ed Fund I learned about poverty, drugs, and the misery of kids scrambling to survive. They are the real heroes, that they were able to make changes and be successful. My challenges have come from inside myself, trying to grow and to develop a certain integrity. At this age and with the practice of meditation there is a proclivity to be drawn more deeply into an interior life, and I'm trying to balance that with time with my husband and grandchildren and all the stuff of daily life."

With her ever-creative mind, Glady expanded on a workshop she developed for LifePlan in a new venture called Building Trust Groups. It was aimed at men and women looking for a way to connect with people and develop what she calls intentional friendships. She found that many people had lost the way to make friends, that after losing friendships through moving, being ejected from a job, or making a friend of someone who was so busy, they would feel rejected.

"People go through life like we're all on our own planets, so rushed and agenda-ridden. We meet and know we have an affinity but there's no chance to really connect at a slower pace—you know, the way people in a country town might have done, where you hung around on the back porch. I am not interested in a social group, so I just picked a few people and suggested that we get together intentionally. I have a number of these groups, and they are so enriching. We meet for lunch and talk about anything. Everyone checks in and it goes from there. It can be sobering or hilarious, but it creates a tremendous bond. There is a sense of commonality, though we live our lives on these different trails, and it finally surfaces this humanness that we all share. At this time in life I have grown into gratitude for living, for being well, and appreciation for what deep friendship gives. It's like a root system; you are able to connect underneath the ground. Friendship truly is the warm hearth in a cold universe."

ACKNOWLEDGMENTS

My love and deepest thanks to each of the wild, wise, dynamic women whose voices you have heard in this book, many of whom I am fortunate to know as friends. They opened themselves generously to share their stories and insights, trials and triumphs, and in doing so confirmed my belief that life holds glorious possibilities at every stage.

My warmest thanks to Paulette Millichap for believing in and encouraging me to write this book; Bennett Hall for creating the serendipity for Paulette and me to meet; Ross Parsons for his painstaking transcriptions; Aileen Hernandez; Claire Ullman; Patrice Wynne who was so very generous with her contacts and support; Patricia Ellsberg, who provided immediate access to her sister; Shelly Fernandez, Virginia Fowler, Patricia Gaul, David Feinstein, and Bridgett the Britt for organizing schedules and meetings; Daphne for pushing me to start; the community of loving friends who cheered me on; all of my ancestors, and especially my parents, to whom I give thanks every day; my brother Ted, whose wisdom made it easier for me to take the time for this book; all of my spiritual teachers; Christine, for being such a grand partner; and my dear Frank Greene for his hours of listening, encouragement, and loving support.

— GWEN MAZER, 2007

I would like to express my gratitude to the women who put their trust in me to photograph them for this book. I also thank Gwen Mazer for her long friendship and belief in my vision, to Chris Johnson for his emotional and computer support, to Aaron and Louise Rose for their hospitality in New York City, to my son, Casey, to my grandmother, parents, brothers, and sisters, and to my good friends for their unconditional love.

— CHRISTINE ALICINO, 2007

Many of the questions I asked women who participated in *Wise Talk Wild Women* are the kind of questions that you might wish to discuss with a good friend over a long, relaxed conversation. They are questions you might ask yourself in private moments of self-exploration. Your answers may lead to other questions and then to other answers and both may change over time. I offer you these questions to use in the process of further discovery in your own life and unfolding.

1 What do you know now that would have been valuable to you to know as a younger woman?

2 What aspect(s) of your temperament have been challenging (for example, curiosity, anger, jealousy, shyness)? How did they affect you?

3 What experiences, "ah hah moments," have had significant influence on the way you live your life at this age?

4 What inspires and challenges you creatively and intellectually at this time?

5 If you have parented children, what did you learn from them?

6 What were your thoughts and feelings as you approached sixty? How was it different from the thoughts and feelings you had being forty or fifty?

7 How is your age of sixty and beyond different for you than it was for your mother, father, or other elders in your family? What was your experience of their attitudes and behavior?

8 In what ways are your preconceived ideas about age different from your actual experience?

9 Given the demoralizing media and advertising messages about growing older, what is your inner dialogue when you see your image in the mirror?

10 Romance, relationship, partnering, marriage, living together— all are possible at any age. In your experience, is it easier or more difficult to love with trust and acceptance as you age? Why?

11 In your opinion, what qualities make women sensuous and vibrant as they age?

12 How will you leave this world a better place?

13 Perceptions of age are beginning to change, but ageism, especially toward women, is very ingrained in our society. What can we do to create changes in attitudes and perceptions about age?

Take time every day to nurture yourself with silence. It feeds your spirit.

Learn to forgive yourself and others.

Listen to your inner voice and trust it.

Let go of your grievances.

Let go of being a victim.

Remember that living in the past keeps you stuck.

Be in the present. It is the only time there is.

Don't expect others to read your mind. Make your wishes known.

Laugh out loud. It's good for both body and soul.

Spend time with nature.She enlivens your spirit.

Look to yourself for happiness and peace.

Be open to new experiences. Stretch!

Love, honor, and nurture your body. Listen to what it asks you to do.

Find your creative expression and embrace it with abandon.

— G M